REFLECTIONS ON SOLITUDE

and other

ESSAYS

SAMEER GROVER

iUniverse, Inc.
Bloomington

Reflections on Solitude and other Essays

Copyright © 2011 by Sameer Grover

iUniverse books may be ordered through booksellers or by contacting:

iUniverse
1663 Liberty Drive
Bloomington, IN 47403
www.iuniverse.com
1-800-Authors (1-800-288-4677)

Because of the dynamic nature of the Internet, any web addresses or links contained in this book may have changed since publication and may no longer be valid. The views expressed in this work are solely those of the author and do not necessarily reflect the views of the publisher, and the publisher hereby disclaims any responsibility for them.

Any people depicted in stock imagery provided by Thinkstock are models, and such images are being used for illustrative purposes only.

Certain stock imagery © Thinkstock.

ISBN: 978-1-4620-5436-7 (sc)
ISBN: 978-1-4620-5437-4 (e)

Printed in the United States of America

iUniverse rev. date: 11/21/2011

For my Teachers

you have come in many forms,
and have led me to the formless.

Contents

Chapter 1

A Return to Innocence

"I remember my youth and the feeling that will never come back any more - the feeling that I could last forever, outlast the sea, the earth, and all men; the deceitful feeling that lures us on to joys, to perils, to love, to vain effort - to death"
-Joseph Conrad.

As the great Beatle, George Harrison, once said, "All things must pass" - it is only a matter of time before the sea of change washes away that which we hold precious. I remember when I first experienced this realization for myself, this realization that every soul must reach at some time or other, each in its own way, each sacred.

The flowers of my youth blossomed in rich soil. My family lived in a middle class neighbourhood, and although we were not a religious family, my brother and I were raised with an exceptional sense of morality. It was this sense of morality that lent our household an austere atmosphere during those early years.

My story commences at ten years of age, a gentle snowfall cascaded from the heavens, the romantic kind usually reserved for postcards. My friend Neil and I were walking home from school. He reached into his pocket, handing me a piece of Hubba Bubba; in those days, Hubba Bubba was the Rolls Royce of chewing gums. I will never forget what he said next as I popped the gum in my mouth, "Guess what? This pack of gum is stolen."

Revulsion overcame me. I was about to spit the gum onto the concrete, then and there! I said nothing. My weakest point had been struck, my sense of morality had been offended, and I could no longer look in the direction of my friend. I was embarrassed for being friends with a heathen. I was the accomplice of a criminal, a thief, a depraved soul who would burn in hell, be reborn as a chimpanzee or hyena, and rot in the realms of the destitute. I went home that day withdrawn, unable to eat, or even play with my brother, I told my parents I was sick, and went to bed.

As I fell asleep, my sense of revulsion towards Neil was gradually replaced by a feeling akin to awe. He had marched into the store, and stolen a pack of gum. He walked out with a pack of Hubba Bubba for nothing; he spent nothing, paid nothing. He had gotten the gum for free, and he had done so because he willed it so. As I became drowsier, this feeling grew, and entirely swept away my initial feelings of disgust.

A week passed, and the whole time Neil remained in my mind. I couldn't keep my eyes off him at school. He carried a secretive smile on his face, bore a look of valour, giving chocolate bars and packs of gum to all of our classmates. He drew smiles from the girls, and had the respect of the boys. He was a hero, a champion of schoolchildren everywhere, Neil was Robin Hood; he stole from the rich, and gave to the poor.

There is a particular day that remains imprinted in my memory, and it is one that I am likely to never forget. In those days, I, like every other boy in grade five - well, those who had outgrown the "cooties" phase, anyways - had the biggest crush on Samantha. She was the prettiest girl in the entire school, and the object of my boyhood affections. I was waiting outside the cloakroom for Neil after school, while he was talking to a smiling Samantha.

As we were about to leave, Samantha leaned over, giving Neil a long kiss on the cheek. My heart fell out of my chest. I was so enveloped in jealousy that I could not speak to Neil as we walked home. I wanted to walk around with that smile on my face, that secretive look, I wanted to be the Robin Hood of grade five, I wanted Samantha to kiss me. In short, I had an identity complex. I wanted to be Neil.

As we were walking home, Neil ducked into one of the alleyways that coursed between the streets of our neighbourhood. I followed somewhat hesitantly, my parents strictly forbade me from walking through the alleys. If they ever discovered the truth, I was certain to be grounded for a week. But, to show cowardice in front of Neil, and his caution-to-the-wind attitude was not an option, so we kept walking.

About halfway down the alley, Neil stopped, pulled off his backpack, and set it on the ground. He reached in, and handed me a Twix bar. I glanced into his open bag, and saw a dozen chocolate bars and another dozen packs of gum, taunting me from within. This was the largest single bounty I had ever seen! Dumbstruck, I asked, "Did you...did you, steal, all of that?"

"Well, you make it sound as if I did something bad, or something like that," he replied. "The store has so many chocolate bars, and packs of bubble gum, so I took a few, so what?"

More than his words, it was the grandeur with which he spoke that remains imbedded in me to this day. That evening, I returned home in a jovial mood, falling asleep swiftly and easily, conviction gripped me in its vice, I knew with sound resolution what I was going to do in the morning.

The morning was cold. I walked into the 7-Eleven around eight thirty, half-an-hour before school started, and there were several other customers in the store when I entered. An overweight, German woman was working the cash register. I nervously strolled down the comic book aisle and looked through the selection - Superman, Batman, Wonder Woman, The Green Hornet - my mind was elsewhere. I gathered my nerves, and sauntered over to the candy aisle.

The cashier was reading a magazine, and paying me no attention whatsoever. I could have purchased what I was going to steal, my parents gave me a healthy allowance, and I only spent it on the odd comic book or pack of baseball cards. I had the money, but, today was different; today, I wasn't going to buy anything. My fate was etched in stone. I took a final glance at the cashier; she was absorbed in the latest issue of *Seventeen* magazine.

My hand reached down for the cherry flavoured Hubba Bubba, seemingly of its own accord, sliding the pack of gum up the arm of my coat. I felt like running. What was I doing? For a brief moment, I was going to remove the gum from my sleeve, and return it to its rightful owner, the box.

I walked back up the candy aisle, and turned the corner, heading straight for the door. The cashier looked at me, her gaze catching mine, this moment lasted centuries.

She knew that I was a thief, she saw me slide the gum into my sleeve, and up the arm of my coat. She knew that I was guilty. She nodded her head, and smiled, telling me to have a swell day. I did not say a word. I did not even smile. I exited the store with a horror stricken expression on my face.

After arriving safely at the schoolyard, I popped the first piece of tainted gum into my mouth. Every single chew was accompanied by shameful guilt. I was now, too, a heathen, a depraved soul. I had disavowed Father and Mother, and everything sacred; I had broken the code of morality that governed our household. I no longer belonged to the bright, happy, world of my parents and brother.

I now belonged to a much darker world, a world of thieves and criminals. However, somewhere in the dark recesses of my heart, a pleasurable sensation accompanied my shame, in some deluded way, I now felt superior to my parents and their world. Amidst these conflicting emotions arose a snowballing fear:, surely, my parents would read the guilty expression in my eyes; surely, they would know I was a criminal. My teachers would know, the other schoolchildren would know; Neil would know; Samantha would know; surely, everyone would know.

The principal would summon me to his office, and pronounce that I was expelled. My parents would send me to military school. Surely, I was doomed. My face would be on the front page of the newspapers, "Ten-year old thief sent to boot camp."

Yet, nothing of the sort happened. Life carried on, pretty much as usual. I was now, however, accompanied by my conscience wherever I went. By day, it was my haunting shadow; by night, the Devil himself terrorized my sleep. I wanted to die, then and there. I was waiting for the angel of mercy; my appointment book was ready. I knew deep down, however, that, in the end, I would overcome my shameful guilt. I knew that I would repent and be forgiven, and I knew that I would forgive myself, for, ultimately, this was the forgiveness that mattered.

When my own conscience was appeased, and had come to terms with my actions, I would smile again, and a certain amount of innocence would return to me. But, it would no longer be the same. I had tasted the forbidden fruit, and I had liked it. I knew that I would steal again, and that I would transgress the line of morality once more, many times more, in fact.

The looking glass of my childhood years was shattered. I was empty, a feeling with which I would become acquainted over the years to come. As George said, "All things must pass," the waves rise and fall, and the seasons change without end; left to the master alchemist of time, so do the seasons of our lives. The springtime of my youth faded away too soon, the evanescence of a dying flame, leaving its fragrance behind to waft in the autumn breeze. The flowers will return in the springtime. Fresh scents will permeate the air, purity will be restored, and all will be forgiven.

Conrad, Joseph. *Youth, a Narrative, and Two Other Stories.* London: Penguin Books, 1975. Print.

Harrison, George. *All Things Must Pass.* Apple, 1970. CD.

Chapter 2

Bridging the Gap between Mathematics and Mysticism

Mysticism has gone hand in hand with mathematics since the beginning of time, that is, if time can be said to have a beginning. The greatest mathematicians have always had profound mystical beliefs. Their numbers include Pythagoras, Leibniz, Fourier, Laplace, Pascal, Kepler, Ptolemy, Euclid, Plato, and Gödel. Virtually everywhere, mysticism is thought of as the mysterious occult or the word conjures imagery of witchcraft. Mysticism can be experienced as the existence of realities beyond perceptual apprehension, realities that are directly accessible by subjective experience.

Essentially, mystical tradition does not adhere to any philosophy; rather, it is the direct apprehension of one's personal identity with God. The central teaching of mysticism is that reality is one. According to mystics throughout time, the road to enlightenment can only be walked along the path of meditation. Through this type of practice one can associate oneself with the cosmic mind which is in fact everywhere, contrary to the popular belief that the mind is localized to the brain.

The 20th century mathematician Kurt Gödel offers this method on how best to experience the cosmic mind directly. He asserts that the first thing that needs to be done is for the senses to be closed off by lying or sitting in a quiet place. He emphasizes that it is a mistake to allow everyday reality to condition possibility, and only to imagine the combinations and permutations of physical objects the mind is truly capable of directly experiencing. Only by closing off one's senses can one leave the finite behind and proceed towards the infinite. Gödel claims that the ultimate goal of all philosophy is perception of the absolute.

Through such practice, it is possible for one to detach oneself from physical reality and to enter into the realm of God, where space and time cease to exist altogether, and everything is one. This reality can only be grasped through intuition rather than through logical reasoning methods. Bertrand Russell asserts there are four main characteristics of mysticism.\

(i) <u>Intuition is a direct way of knowing</u>. David Suzuki calls this way of knowing the world prajna. This type of way of knowing can neither be taught nor dissertated; rather, it is communicated through a mystical grasping of the world in its unity.

(ii) <u>A belief in the unity of all things</u>. In other words, it is the refusal to admit opposition or division anywhere. Mystics throughout history have asserted that all of reality is in fact a cosmic dance. In Hinduism, the dance is called maya, it is the illusion of the separateness of all things; to pierce the veil of maya is to see through the illusion and directly perceive the infinite.

(iii) <u>All evil is mere appearance</u>. It is an illusion produced by the divisions and oppositions of the analytical mind. When unified with the cosmic mind, there is no such thing as evil, and it is our sense of separation that allows for the illusion of evil to exist. Mysticism does not maintain that such things as cruelty are good, rather it denies that they are real, they belong to the lower world of phantoms from which we are to be liberated by the insight of vision. The mystic lives in full light of this vision: what others dimly seek, he knows with a knowledge beside which all other knowledge is ignorance.

(iv) <u>The denial of the reality of time</u>. The importance of time is theoretical, existing only in relation to our desires, rather than to knowledge of truth. Even though time can seem real, to realize, in both thought and feeling, the unimportance of time is the gateway to wisdom. In fact, this thought, which has been known to mystics throughout the centuries, was truly proven when Albert Einstein published his Relativity Theory.

Relativity Theory asserts that as an object approaches the speed of light time slows down. Virtually all physicists now agree that if an astronaut were to travel to a distant star and return, moving at a velocity close to that of light, he could, in theory, travel thousands of years into the Earth's future. If one were to travel at the speed of light itself, then time would completely stop, and one would be, as they say, "stuck in a moment".

The conjecture now is that tachyons, particles moving faster than light, actually exist. Relativity theory leaves no escape from the fact that anything moving at a velocity faster than the speed of light – or "several multiples of c" as Kevin Spacey's character says in *K-Pax* – would move backwards in time. The implications of the existence of such tachyons are endless, and could pave the way for a real life Delorien to exist in the future, or even the past for that matter. This type of creative development would be the ultimate merger of mysticism and mathematics.

Many of the great names of history have merged their wisdom of mathematics and mysticism. Among them, none ranks higher than Pythagoras. He was at once a wizard and a mathematical icon, and the founder of the Pythagorean School, a mystical sect who dealt with mathematics and philosophy, and it is their work that is frequently credited with bringing about the birth of modern mathematical physics.

While they made advanced leaps and bounds in mathematics, they were best known for the tenet of metempsychosis, another term for reincarnation. Pythagoras is said to have been able to remember many of his past lives as well as having many other "supernatural" powers. They believed that there is one cosmic mind or soul, and that you are alive because a small piece of this soul is imprisoned in your body, and that bit of soul that animates you will animate many other bodies before returning to unity with the one cosmic soul.

The Pythagoreans adhered to a great number of rules and taboos in an effort to bring themselves into closer harmony with the cosmos. Among them were strict vegetarianism and not accepting pay for their teachings. It was hoped that if you could bring yourself into close enough harmony with the one cosmic soul when your body died, the soul that vivified it might return to the source instead of incarnating again.

The Pythagorean School was also where a young Plato learned mathematics after the death of his teacher Socrates. Like Pythagoras, Plato sought the key to the universe in arithmetic and geometry. When asked about the occupation of God, Plato answered that "He geometrizes continually". In fact, Plato believed that the good of geometry is set aside and destroyed when reduced to the world of sense instead of being elevated with the ethereal images of thought, as employed by God for which reason he is always God. He also believed that the study of geometry is a necessary preparation for the study of philosophy. He observed that geometry trained the mind for correct and vigorous thinking. He placed this inscription over his porch "Let no man who is unacquainted with geometry enter here."

Mathematicians in the last 500 years have faced stricter opposition for holding mystical beliefs. Modern sceptics of mysticism are abundant throughout the mathematical world. Twentieth century giants such as Gödel and Einstein come to mind as examples of modern mystics; their mathematical achievements are crowned without their denying the existence of a supreme reality. Despite the scepticism of the scientific community, the fact remains that mathematics and mysticism exist concurrently as necessary requisites for anyone who wishes to adequately comprehend the universe.

Russell, Bertrand. *Mysticism and Logic and Other Essays*. London: G, Allen & Unwin, 1917. Print.

"Maya: Illusion."*The Heart of Hinduism*. ISKCON Communications, 2004. Web. 9 May. 2011.

K-Pax. Dir. Iain Softley. Perf. Kevin Spacey, Jeff Bridges, and Mary McCormack. Universal Pictures, 2001. DVD.

http://www.thalesians.com/finance/index.php/Quotes

Mackey, G. Albert, and Haywood, L. Harry. *Encyclopedia of Freemasonry*. Chicago: The Masonic History Company, 1946. Print.

Riedweg, Christoph. *Pythagoras*. Trans. and Ed. Steven Rendall. New York: Cornell University Press, 2005. Print.

Chapter 3

Visitors in my Guesthouse

Many visitors come to my guesthouse. They may arrive excited or angry, happy or distraught; they may come laughing or screaming, singing or crying. Regardless of their temperament, I greet them all with a smile. I greet them with courtesy, joy, and perfect equanimity. I invite them to stay as long as they please, and they are always free to leave whenever they so desire.

Often, my visitors sit for a while and I listen to them. I listen patiently to whatever it is they have to discuss, and I listen until they have exhausted what they have come to say. Where these travelers go when they leave my guesthouse, I do not know. Nor do I know from whence they came. I only know that when they arrive at my guesthouse they are loved and acknowledged.

When my guesthouse is empty, I rejoice in the pleasure of being. I rejoice in the pure pleasure of emptiness, and of dwelling in the sacred space of being, the still moments in between visitors. I rejoice, as I patiently await another visitor whose journey has led him to the guesthouse of my mind.

Chapter 4

The Way of the Tao

"The journey of a thousand miles begins with a single step."- Lao Tzu

Taoism arose in China during the time of the Han dynasty in the 2nd century BC, as a form of direct opposition to the dominant ideologies of Confucianism; the graceful teachings of Taoism are the very embodiment of a counterculture. The term Tao is literally translated as "the way", and the Tao te Ching, the fundamental canon of Taoism, was written during this epoch, and is attributed to the sage Lao Tzu. The name of Lao Tzu literally translates to mean "old master". Very shortly after the time of Lao Tzu, emerged Chuang Tzu, and he is the second leading figure of contemporary Taoism.

In order to properly assert that Taoism was a counterculture, we must first have a working definition of what is meant by a counterculture; one is given here: "The term 'counterculture' was coined in the 1960s, largely in response to the emergence of middle-class youth movements that questioned the values of the dominant culture." Often, we tend to think only of countercultures in contemporary terms, however, the emergence of

Taoism in ancient China can easily be seen as that of a counterculture, since it directly questioned the values of the Confucian culture that was prevalent at the time. This stark contrast between the two philosophical doctrines is well illustrated here, "in place of the Confucian concern for things worldly and human, it (Taoism) holds out a vision of other, transcendental worlds of the spirit."

There are three defining principles of a counterculture, and they are as follows:

(1) Countercultures assign primacy to individuality at the expense of social conventions and governmental constraints.

(2) Countercultures challenge authoritarianism in both obvious and subtle forms.

(3) Countercultures embrace individual and social change.

Given this contextual framework, Taoism is the very epitome of what it means to be a counterculture. The first of these defining principles is evident throughout Taoist literature and is best captured by the following quote from J. J. Clarke, author of *Tao of the West*, who finds in Taoism, "a valuing and cultivation of the personal life above service to the state." It must be noted that Taoist individuality is, paradoxically, not primarily concerned with gratification of the ego or self but, rather, simply with following the way within the parameters of one's very own life, and living in harmony and accord with nature.

The second defining principle, again, is resolute throughout Taoist literature and is best depicted through the following passage: "When they lose their sense of awe, people turn to religion. When they no longer trust themselves, they begin to depend upon authority." The third and final of these defining characteristics is extremely pertinent to the Taoist doctrine; for, embracing change is the central tenet of Taoism. This is well demonstrated by the terminology "go with the flow"; for this popular sixties aphorism was a gift from Taoism.

The Tao is marked by a tendency towards acceptance and yielding, an absence of strife or coercion, and of living in a manner that is completely spontaneous and effortless. This approach to action is often expressed in terms of doing nothing or of doing nothing that is unnatural or not within "the way"; this mode of action is called *Wu Wei*. *Wu Wei* literally translates as doing nothing, however, a more precise context is provided by Benjamin Hoff: "Literally, *Wu Wei* means 'without doing, causing, or making.' But practically speaking, it means without meddlesome, combative or egotistical effort." This concept of Wu Wei as a natural state of being is further extrapolated upon by Hoff: "The efficiency of *Wu Wei* is like that of water flowing over and around the rocks in its path - not the mechanical, straight-line approach that usually ends up short-circuiting natural laws, but one that evolves from an inner sensitivity to the natural rhythm of things."

The notion of *Wu Wei*, this mode of effortless action, is in direct contradiction to the Confucian ideals of intellectual analysis and concerted effort, and here lies one of the strong points of divergence between Confucianism and Taoism. Whereas in Confucianism, strong and determined action is seen as noble and worthy, in Taoism it is viewed as unnatural, as going against the harmony of nature, or as constricting "the way".

Another important element of Taoism is that of *P'u* or the Uncarved Block, which implies that all things are truly at their best when they are viewed in their original essence. This, too, is well explained by Hoff: "The essence of the principle of the Uncarved Block is that things in their original simplicity contain their own natural power, power that is easily spoiled and lost when that simplicity is changed."

This notion of *P'u* is of the utmost importance in the doctrine of Taoism, as it is the foundation for the notion of emptiness as being the most desirable state of existence and of intellectual thought as being a great limitation to the gateway of truth. This notion of emptiness and clarity is captured well by Hoff: "It's rather significant that the Taoist ideal is that of the still, calm, reflecting 'mirror-mind' of the Uncarved Block."

The idea that the Tao cannot be known through scholarship or intellect is well illustrated in the following passage from Hoff: "A well frog cannot imagine the ocean, nor can a summer insect conceive of ice. How then can a scholar understand the Tao? He is restricted by his own learning."

Perhaps, this notion of the uncarved block as original simplicity is, however, best captured by the following passage from Lao Tzu:

"Do away with sageliness, discard knowledge,
And the people will benefit a hundredfold.
Do away with humaneness, discard rightness,
And the people will once more be filial and loving.
Dispense cleverness, discard profit,
And there will be no more bandits and thieves.

These three, to be regarded as ornaments, are insufficient.
Therefore let the people have something to cling to:
Manifest plainness,
Embrace uncarved wood,
Diminish selfishness,
Reduce desires."

The free-spirited doctrine of the Tao is, at once, light-hearted and humorous, and this can especially be seen in comparison with the stern elements of Confucianism. This light-hearted and humorous element is often a characteristic of countercultural movements: "Counterculturalists tend to be jokers, bohemians, and libertines… Humour was an instrument for transmitting profound wisdom in the teaching tales of Taoism, Sufism and Zen. The stories from all these traditions similarly rely on existential, mind-twisting punch lines to alter the listener's perceptions."

This humorous element of the Taoist counterculture was frequently used to demonstrate the follies of the Confucian hierarchies and socio-political ideologies, as observed here: "He who steals a belt buckle pays with his life; he who steals a state gets to be a feudal lord."

The existential, mind-altering component of Taoist humor is well exemplified by the story of Zhuang Zhou,

Once Zhuang Zhou dreamed he was a butterfly. A butterfly fluttering happily around - was he revealing what he himself meant to be? He knew nothing of Zhou. All at once awakening, there suddenly he was - Zhou. But he didn't know if he was Zhou having dreamed he was a butterfly or a butterfly dreaming he was Zhou.

Between Zhou and the butterfly there must surely be some distinction. This is known as the transformation of things.

Taoism is one of the few contemporary religions or philosophies where female characteristics are seen as superior to those of the male. The Taoist notions of spontaneity, yielding, and submission to the natural order are tendencies that are generally associated with the female. This notion of these female-associated characteristics as being superior to those of the male is exemplified throughout the Tao te Ching, however, perhaps, best here: "Nothing in the world is as soft and yielding as water. Yet for dissolving the hard and inflexible, nothing can surpass it. The soft overcomes the hard; the gentle overcomes the rigid."

Indeed, there is no room in the Taoist doctrine for the traditionally male-associated characteristics of force, exaggerated effort, and rational analysis; these tendencies were left for Confucianism. This notion of the yielding qualities of the female as being superior to the exerting ones of the male are also illustrated in the Taoist advice to the ruling and institutions of the time and is shown here:

"A large state is the effluence of a river,
Confluence of the world,
Female of the world.
Through stillness the female always overcomes the male.
Through stillness she submits.
Thus, by submitting, a large state wins a small one,
And a small state, by submitting to a large state,
Wins the large state.

Thus one submits in order to win,
The other submits in order to be won.
The large state only wants to nourish the people
as a whole.
The small state only wants to enter the service
of others.
Each getting what it wants, it is right to submit."

Much of the teachings of the Tao were written in order to advise the ruling institutions of the time. For centuries, most Chinese rulers employed a contingent of Taoist advisors. The yielding nature of the Tao and the lack of attachment to fixed structures, order, and hierarchy were central to the political beliefs of these ruling institutions. This concept is well illustrated here: "Let go the fixed plans and concepts, and the world will govern itself … The more prohibitions you have, the less virtuous people will be. The more weapons you have, the less secure people will be. The more subsidies you have, the less self-reliant people will be. Therefore the Master says: I let go of the law, and people become honest."

Taoist politics can, then, be classified as anarchistic in nature. The most common misconception concerning anarchist politics is demonstrated here: "The common belief is that an anarchist is a person who advocates 'no government.' This is generally true, but the phrase 'no governor' is more exact, since there may be agreed-upon rules (preferably by consensus) and ways of enforcing those rules when absolutely necessary."

It can then be seen that the Taoist doctrine and teachings epitomize the very nature of what it means to be a counterculture. Their embrace of change, focus on individuality, and challenge of the dominant Confucian ideals of the time fit perfectly into the contextual framework of a counterculture. The libertine spirit of the Tao, along with its light-hearted, often humorous and, above all else, yielding and spontaneous nature are in stark contrast with the regimented, hierarchical, structured, and rigid Confucian ideals that permeated Chinese thought prior to the arrival of the Tao. The emphasis of the Tao on *Wu Wei*, on doing nothing, performing effortless action, and maintaining harmony with nature provides it with an element of feeling and warmth that is lacking in Confucian thought. The notion of *P'uh*, of the Uncarved Block, provides an insight into the true nature of wisdom; a wisdom that is distant, if not entirely removed, from the analytical methodologies of Confucianism. The political dimensions of the Tao demonstrate that ruling institutions should behave in a similar manner to the Taoist sage; to be free and yielding, spontaneous and graceful, this is the essential nature of the Tao, and to embrace change on a personal level provides life with its ultimate meaning. To paraphrase Lao Tzu, "Conquering others requires force while conquering the self requires strength."

http://www.quotationspage.com/quote/24004.html

http://www.olemiss.edu/courses/inst203/debary60iv.pdf

Goffman, Ken, and Dan Joy. *Counterculture Through the Ages: From Abraham to Acid House.* New York: Villard Books, 2005. Print.

Clark, J.J. *The Tao of the West.* London: Routledge, 2000. Print.

Lao Tzu. *Tao Te Ching.* Trans. and Ed. Gia-Fu Feng, and Jane English. New York: Vintage Books, 1972. Print.

Lao Tzu. *Lao-tzu's Taoteching.* Trans. and Ed. Red Pine. San Francisco, Mercury House, 1996. Print.

Lao Tzu. *Tao Te Ching.* Trans. and Ed. Stephen Mitchell. New York: HarperPerennial, 1992. Print.

Bary de, WM. Theodore, and Irene Bloom, ed. *Sources of Chinese Tradition.* New York: Columbia University Press, 1999. Print.

Lao Tzu. *Tao Te Ching.* Trans. and Ed. D.C. Lau. London: Penguin Books, 1963. Print.

Hoff, Benjamin, and Earnest H. Shepard. *The Tao of Pooh.* New York: Dutton, 1982. Print.

Chapter 5

An Analysis of the Doctrine of Anatman in the Subtext of Mahayana Buddhism

The focus of this essay is to examine the doctrine of 'no soul' (anatman in Sanskrit, anatta in Pali) within the context of Mahayana Buddhism. "The Buddha's doctrine of anatman literally means no atman: there is no immortal, unchanging self or soul." In order to conduct a precise analysis of this doctrine we will examine it in relation to the Buddhist doctrines of the five aggregates and conditioned genesis, in addition to the common Buddhist ideas of impermanence, emptiness, and Universal Buddha Nature. The five aggregates and conditioned genesis rest at the core of Mahayana Buddhism, and are of the utmost importance in understanding the philosophy of anatman. "The doctrine of anatta or no-soul is the natural result of, or corollary to, the analysis of the Five Aggregates and the teaching of conditioned genesis."

During this essay we will not discuss the rise and popularization of Buddhism in China; rather we will focus entirely on the philosophical principles of the doctrine of anatman within the context of Mahayana Buddhism. While the doctrine of "no soul" is a central tenet to the philosophy of Mahayana Buddhism, it should be duly noted that the idea is common to Hinayana Buddhism as well: "The negation of an imperishable Atman (soul) is the common characteristic of all dogmatic systems of the Lesser (Hinayana) as well as the Great Vehicle (Mahayana), and, there is, therefore, no reason to assume that Buddhist tradition which is in complete agreement on this point has deviated from the Buddha's original teaching."

A fundamental premise of Buddhism is that the nature of existence is changing; that which exists at one moment, does not exist at the next moment. This fundamental premise of impermanence is the underlying principle behind the four noble truths of Buddhism. The four noble truths are "(1) all life is inevitably sorrowful (2) sorrow is due to craving (3) sorrow can only be stopped by the stopping of craving, and (4) this can be done by a course of carefully disciplined conduct."

It can be seen, then, how the notion of impermanence has formulated Buddhist thought since its birth, and how the removal of attachment to objects of impermanence can alleviate suffering. At the root of all suffering lies the notion of self and it is, thus, that the loss of this "self" leads one to enlightenment. The question naturally arises, if there is no self and if everything is impermanent then what really exists? According to the Buddha's teachings the only things that exist are momentary states called dharmas (dhamma in Pali), "a person is a temporary collection of constantly changing dharmas."

In Buddhism there are five of these that constitute a person, these are also known as the five aggregates. According to this principle everything is made up of the five aggregates. These aggregates are form, sensation, perception, will or karmic predisposition, and consciousness. "The individual is made up of a combination of the five components, which are never the same from one moment to the next, and therefore the individual's whole being is in a state of constant flux." The self is usually perceived as the permanent center linking these aggregates. The Buddha said that every human experience can be explained in terms of the five aggregates, and, therefore, there is no self behind the experience. "Thus there is neither evidence nor need for an underlying 'self' to account fully for human experience."

According to the doctrine of conditioned genesis, nothing in the world is absolute; everything is relative and interdependent. Life and its cessation can be explained in the following detailed formula of conditioned genesis: "1. Through ignorance are conditioned volitional actions or karma-formulations 2. Through volitional actions is conditioned consciousness 3. Through consciousness are conditioned mental and physical phenomena 4. Through mental and physical phenomena are conditioned the six faculties (i.e. five physical sense-organs and mind) 5. Through the six faculties is conditioned (sensorial and mental) contact 6. Through (sensorial and mental) contact is conditioned sensation 7. Through sensation is conditioned desire ('thirst') 8. Through desire ('thirst') is conditioned clinging 9. Through clinging is conditioned the process of becoming 10. Through the process of becoming is conditioned birth 11. Through birth are conditioned decay, death, lamentation, pain, etc."

It must be remembered, too, that the process of conditioned genesis is cyclical, and that the wheel of samsara leads from death back to birth again. According to Buddhist doctrine - both Mahayana and Hinayana - this process not only explains how life arises, exists, and continues, but also how it ceases, thereby providing the path to nirvana. One of the basic principles of Mahayana Buddhism is that all things are interdependent, and this can be seen in the early Buddhist doctrine of 'dependent origination'. The Indian philosopher Nagarjuna (2nd.), one of the foremost and greatest Mahayana thinkers, made the following statement, "emptiness is dependent origination."

In other words this notion of all things being interdependent is the root of emptiness. If everything is interdependent and always changing, then how can there be any permanent self? Thus emptiness really means "emptiness of self nature." This concept of emptiness (kong in Sanskrit) is actually an expression of the concept of anatman applied to all things and is one of the most fundamentally important Mahayana principles.

We are now in a position to examine the philosophical principle, made new by Mahayana, of "Universal Buddha Nature". It is this central Mahayana principle that makes the possibility of enlightenment available to all people. The premise that enlightenment is possible for all sentient beings, not just monks and nuns living in monasteries, is one of the major philosophical reasons why Mahayana Buddhism had become widely accepted in China. In other words, all sentient beings (and according to later Mahayana thinkers also inanimate objects) are manifestations of Buddhahood. Since emptiness means the lack of independence, to state it positively we can say that emptiness means interdependence.

It follows therefore that if all things are fundamentally interdependent, then all things share the same nature as bodhisattvas. This concept of Universal Buddha Nature can, indeed, be used to show that the self is empty and that all things are, in fact, interdependent and impermanent, lacking autonomous nature and identity of any sort. Following this line of reasoning, it can be shown that samsara and nirvana are, too, interdependent and share the same nature. In fact, both are fundamentally empty and cannot be distinct from one another. According to Nagarjuna there is no difference between samsara and nirvana; this statement appears paradoxical because the original meaning of nirvana was liberation from the bondage of samsara.

According to this line of reasoning, we may say that nirvana is the true nature of samsara, and samsara that of nirvana, such that, in fact, there is no duality. Both of these would then be fundamentally empty in nature, as would the notion of atman. Thus, this "self" and all that exists share the same fundamentally empty nature. While the Buddha, himself, would not acknowledge the existence of a self, he would neither explicitly deny it either, for fear of being misunderstood as an annihilationist. This can be seen through the story of the wanderer named Vacchagotta who came to see The Buddha in order to inquire about the nature of the self. "Vacchagotta comes to The Buddha and asks: 'Venerable Gotama, is there an Atman?' The Buddha is silent. 'Then Venerable Gotama, is there no Atman?' Again The Buddha is silent. Vacchagotta gets up and goes away.'"

After the wanderer had left, Ananda, The Buddha's chief disciple, asked him why he did not answer Vacchagotta's question. The Buddha then told Ananda that if he had answered that there is indeed a permanent and unchanging self he would have been supporting those ascetics of the time who followed the eternalist theory. Furthermore, this answer would not have been in accordance with his knowledge and understanding of impermanence, the five aggregates, and conditioned genesis. Had he answered that there is no self or no Atman then he would have been supporting those ascetics who followed the annihilationist theory, and the poor wanderer would have become confused, thinking that previously he had a self that was now no longer. Therefore out of great compassion for the wanderer, and from the depths of his own understanding, The Buddha chose silence as the best answer.

We have now examined in depth, the nature and foundation of the doctrine of anatman in Mahayana Buddhism. It is clear that this philosophy does not exist independent of other Buddhist philosophies and doctrines; rather, they are all intertwined as logical extensions of one another. According to conditioned genesis, the only things that really exist are the five aggregates (form, sensation, perception, will or karmic disposition, and consciousness) and these aggregates are momentary states that are devoid of self. The nature of existence can, then, be explained from the cyclical process of conditioned genesis, and it is through this that the doctrine of anatman is best illustrated within the context of Mahayana Buddhism.

Bary de, WM. Theodore, and Irene Bloom, ed. *Sources of Chinese Tradition*. New York: Columbia University Press, 1999. Print.

Rahula, Walpola. *What the Buddha Taught*. New York: Grove Press, 1974. Print.

Chapter 6

Always

I gazed dreamily out of the window of the train, enraptured by the rolling countryside. I straightened in my seat, shifted my gaze, and allowed it to meander about the train, momentarily landing this way and that, pausing and lingering, and then continuing to wander. It was as if my eyes were moving of their own accord, searching for something. I knew not what I was looking for, only that there was something for which I was looking.

My gaze fell upon several well-dressed men and women wearing formal business attire with their briefcases resting in their laps. They were smiling; yet, their smiles seemed false, as if their smiles were masking a profound suffering within them. My gaze then fell upon a younger crowd that was chattering boisterously; although certainly not insincere, their laughter seemed to be artificial, a well-rehearsed charade designed to disguise the suffering that lay at the very core of their being.

My eyes then fell upon an elderly couple lightly holding hands, with grim looks of worry and discontent spelled on their faces. My gaze continued to wander, my eyes landing on the young and the elderly, the rich and the poor, the infirm and the healthy. Everywhere I looked

I saw this suffering, and the realization began to dawn on me that life itself is fraught with suffering.

I closed my eyes, and took several deep breaths from my abdomen, breaths that came as naturally as the wind itself, and then opened my eyes once more with my gaze immediately falling upon a woman that was beautiful beyond measure. The beauty this woman radiated was greater than any that I had ever seen in my life to date. The beauty that attracted me so, was not an outward beauty, rather, it was an inward beauty; it was as if this woman glowed, emitted a golden light, the type that is said to envelope the beings of the great sages, and, in fact, in varying degrees envelopes all people.

She sat perfectly still, unflinching, the most peaceful presence that I had yet to come across in my young life. Even from a distance, I noticed the twinkle in her starry eyes, a twinkle that suggested a childlike nature, one of innocence and purity, untainted and unscathed by the habits of worldly life.

The train continued on, passing several more stops before I mustered up the courage to rise from my seat and approach this enchanting woman. As I moved towards her, an incredible feeling of lightness of being overcame me. I timidly sat in the seat facing the woman, with neither of us speaking a word. I raised my eyes to meet hers, and in that instant all notions of time had stopped, leaving me speechless. "Excuse me Jeremy, do you know what time it is?" the woman asked.

She knew my name! How on earth did this woman, this complete stranger, know my name?

"Um," I stammered, disarmed, as I mechanically pulled out my old pocket-watch. "It's 10:15."

The woman's eyes met mine again, her gaze penetrating deep into the core of my being as she smiled, a childlike smile. "The time is now," she said, her voice as gentle as an ocean breeze. "The time is always now, and it always will be now, never forget that, Jeremy."

I stared in disbelief at the modern day mystic seated before me on the train. "How do you know my name?" I asked, perplexed.

She gazed ever deeper into my being. "Names are meaningless, they are labels that keep us from seeing our interconnectedness, and they keep us from seeing the unified nature of our being. If you must really know the truth Jeremy, at the deepest and most fundamental level of our nature, it is that I *am* you."

"You *are* me… are you telepathic or something like that?" I asked, hoping not to sound too embarrassed.

The woman began to laugh. Her laughter could not help but bring a smile to my face. "Yes Jeremy, of course, I am telepathic. Aren't we all?" she asked, before continuing. "Telepathy is perfectly natural. The key is to quiet your mind, and free it from the distractions that usually preoccupy it. It has been said that there are windows through which we can enter into each other's minds, but if no walls existed, then why do we need to erect windows?"

"Where I live, Jeremy, there is no distinction between you and I," she continued. "There are no walls between our minds, nor between our hearts, so telepathy, as you call it, is just my way of tapping into a different part of my own consciousness, your consciousness."

I continued to stare in disbelief, when, all of a sudden, the thought struck me like a hammer to the head of a nail, this woman was free from suffering. Unlike all of the other people that I had encountered in this life, this woman was entirely free from suffering. She had liberated herself and, in so doing, held the capacity to help others to liberate themselves.

The woman rose slowly to leave the train, she rose as gracefully as the morning sun.

"Will I ever see you again?" I asked sheepishly.

The woman laughed her melodious laugh that I had already come to love. "I am here Jeremy, all of the time. It is up to you to see me. I have ten thousand different names and I come in ten thousand different forms. My face can be seen in the innocent eyes of a child, in the heart of a snowflake, and in the glory of the setting sun. My voice can be heard in the song of a swan, in the roaring of an ocean tide, and in a whispering wind. My breath is the very breath of life itself. I am here and now, in every single moment I am there, all you have to do is choose to see me; wherever you are Jeremy, that is where I am, and that is where you will find me."

"Always?" I asked.

The woman nodded her head as she departed the train. "Always."

Chapter 7

An Indian Tale

In Indian culture, the extended family is usually close-knit. My cousins and I have viewed each other more along the lines of siblings than as cousins. In this manner, I have many brothers and sisters, as well as nieces and nephews, aunts and uncles, from my extended family, and whom I had not seen in about six-and-a-half years, prior to embarking on my journey. This journey provided me with the opportunity to reunite with my family, to attend my cousin-sister D's wedding, and to spend some time in some of the most amazing places that this planet has to offer a man like myself.

My journey began as many of my journeys have, in the presence of my saintly friend Venerable T. T. Dhammo; his presence seems to set my journeys off on the right foot. Venerable Dhammo dropped me off at Pearson International Airport in Toronto, where I boarded a flight for Amsterdam. On the flight, I happened to be sitting next to a man named S, who is a yoga teacher and Ayurvedic practitioner. He gave me a crash course in Ayurvedic healing and medicine on the flight to Amsterdam, and he informed me that his services normally would cost in the range of $60/ hour.

Schiphol Airport in Amsterdam is one of my favourite transit locations, as it has a meditation area in the airport. So, in transition, I had a good hour-long yoga session with S which loosened me up for the subsequent flight to Delhi. I arrived in Delhi on February 5th, and upon arrival, my uncle V and cousin-brother K picked me up.

My first day in Delhi was certainly eventful. K and I began the day by receiving Ayurvedic massages. We were each treated to two practitioners simultaneously working on us, and by the end of the treatment, were absolutely covered in medicinal oil. There, too, happened to be a symposium on Building a Culture of Peace around the corner from my uncle's place, so after our massages we attended the conference. It was a nice experience to share stories with the folks in Delhi, who are doing some amazing work to help promote a culture of peace for the children of India.

One heart-warming practice that I witnessed is the freedom of holding hands. One frequently finds two men holding hands, or two women holding hands, in a non-romantic way; this palpable gesture of affection is greatly feared in Western culture. One of my favourite activities while staying in India is drinking freshly-squeezed juice by the road side. For the equivalent of about twenty-five cents you can pick up a tall glass of freshly-squeezed orange juice or mixed fruit juice. My father since informed me that this is something I also used to enjoy doing when I visited India as a child.

On the morning of February 10th, after four full days in Delhi catching up with family, I took a four-hour train ride north to Chandigarh where my aunt lives. On the train ride, I noticed many families living in dilapidated brick shanties lining the train tracks. We in North America know nothing of abject poverty; our prison cells would have been luxurious accommodations for these people. Yet, despite their destitute living conditions, the smiles on their faces were beaming and radiant. They might well have been happy enough, just as they were.

Chandigarh is a beautiful city, with a large lake adorning the centre of the college-town. I had the opportunity to take a leisurely stroll along the lake with my aunt, and also to visit its world-famous rock garden, which is, indeed, quite fascinating. After two days in Chandigarh, on the morning of February the 12th, I departed by car for Dharamsala, the meditation capital of the world.

The name Dharamsala translates from Sanskrit to mean "the rest house", and it is here that His Holiness (H.H.) the Dalai Lama and the Tibetan community-in-exile make their home. McLeod Ganj, also known as Upper Dharamsala, or Little Lhasa, is where Namgyal Monastery, the home of His Holiness, is located. McLeod Ganj is also the hotbed for courses in meditation, yoga, Reiki, and other spiritual practices.

McLeod Ganj is a cultural cornucopia of Westerners, Tibetans, and Indians, who have all come together with the goal of furthering their spiritual attainments. It is quietly nestled in the Himalayas at about 2100 metres above sea level. The roads leading up to Dharamsala are steep, winding, and steadily ascending, with monkeys playfully lining the hillside.

I was introduced to the kindness of the Tibetan people on my first night in McLeod Ganj, when I entered a restaurant, and naively sat at a table alone; a Buddhist monk waved for me to come and sit with him and his friend. This monk's name was K P, and he explained to me in great detail the dire straits of the Tibetan people.

He recounted how, in 2005, he made the arduous journey from Tibet to India with several others.

They hiked continuously through the Himalayas for one month from Lhasa to Dharamsala, walking by night and sleeping in caves by day, lest they be captured and killed by the Chinese military patrolling the area. They ate a certain species of small plant (the name of which escapes me now) that grows in this most unfriendly of terrains. Many Tibetans die while undertaking this journey each year whether due to frostbite, starvation, or capture at the hands of the Chinese.

H. H. the Dalai Lama himself was on a journey abroad at this time – the man travels like a rock star – nonetheless, I had the pleasure of visiting Namgyal Monastery and seeing his home. At the Dalai Lama monastery and the Tibetan museum, I had the opportunity to learn further of the injustices that are currently happening in Tibet itself. Many Tibetans who have remained in their homeland, especially the monks and nuns, are regularly beaten by the Chinese police for the open practice of their religion and culture. All of human behaviour is motivated by one of the two emotions, either fear or love, and it is a psychology of fear that causes one being to inflict harm upon another.

Also while in McLeod Ganj, I completed my second degree of Reiki under the tutelage of a renowned Master. I also had a chance to immerse myself in meditation, and am grateful to my friends at Dhamma Sikhara, the Vipassana Meditation Centre, for keeping the centre open for me to meditate at my leisure. I also had the honour of visiting the offices of the Tibetan Government in Exile, in Lower Dharamsala, and talking to some of the officials working there. Dharamsala is a tranquil abode that fully lives up to its name, and is absolutely the ideal place for furthering one's spiritual practice. It is with great enthusiasm that I look forward to returning to Dharamsala.

From McLeod Ganj I took a car to Jammu, a five-hour drive away, and this is my father's birthplace. Hence, it was of great personal significance for me to visit there. I arrived on the evening of Friday the 20th, and had the full day of Saturday the 21st to spend in Jammu. I flew back to Delhi on the following day, Sunday, the 22nd, to partake in the week-long wedding festivities of my cousin-sister D.

D moved to the United Kingdom from India about five years ago where she attended teacher's college, and subsequently took a job as a teacher. While there she met a wonderful young man named J; their wedding was to take place on the evening of Friday, February 27th. About a dozen of J's closest family and friends accompanied him from the U. K. to India.

The festive nature of Indian weddings is incomparable in scope, and this one was certainly no exception; D and J's wedding was one wild week-long celebration. The week began innocuously enough with a small gathering at my uncle V's place- D's father- on the Monday evening. Wednesday evening was the ring ceremony, and this featured an outdoor celebration that included dancing, flowers, and food.

The following day was the henna ceremony where D had her body painted in intricate designs using henna paint. Many of the others in attendance, both men and women, had their hands or parts of their arms painted in henna. I had a gallant peacock painted on my left hand. This night also featured dancing, flowers, and food: the three staples of any Indian gathering.

Finally, the night everyone had been waiting for had arrived. J was elegantly handsome in his traditional Indian garb, D was stunning in her colourful attire, and the night once more featured dancing, flowers, and food; we didn't get to sleep until well past 5 am. After the wedding, I took a day of reprieve before heading for Rishikesh.

If Dharamsala is the meditation capital of the world, then Rishikesh is certainly the yoga capital of the world. It was made famous in the Western world in the 1960's by four fellows named John, Paul, George, and Ringo. It is here that the Beatles came to learn yoga and meditation, and composed the majority of the songs from their masterpiece work, The White Album. Rishikesh is considered a holy city by Hindus, and therefore the consumption of alcohol and meat are strictly prohibited.

I was blessed by a wonderful stroke of fortune as I arrived in Rishikesh on March 1st, the same day as the week-long International Yoga Festival (IYF) was beginning. The IYF is the single largest gathering of yogis and yoginis in the world, and this year's event had about five hundred participants. Another wonderful stroke of luck was that I happened to be staying adjacent to Parmarth Niketan, the ashram where the IYF was being held.

I went out for an evening stroll and it is here that I first saw the massive crowd seated by the riverbank of the Ganges, celebrating the opening of the festival. Needless to say, I sat down amongst the crowd on the riverbank and observed the wonderful aarti festival where small oil lamps are sent out into the river as an offering of light back to the Divine source. The Ganges is much cleaner in Rishikesh than in other locations such as Haridwar, even though the two cities are only an hour's drive apart.

The next day I took part in the classes and festivities of the IYF. Throughout the day I met some amazing people from all over the world. One significant person whom I met, and who took a particular liking to me, was J A, a New York Times best-selling author, and she happily gave me words of encouragement as I embarked on my career of authorship.

That evening a great honour was bestowed upon me as I was asked to go on stage and represent Canada at the evening's aarti ceremony. It was with immeasurable gratitude that I represented my country at the largest yoga gathering in the world. Although, I had to leave Rishikesh the next day - due only to the fact that I had a flight back to Canada the day following - attending the festival was an incredible experience and, God-willing, I will be back again in the near future.

I am delighted to have been immersed in the presence of loving people, diverse landscapes, a fascinating culture, and an incomparable spiritual heritage. One thing I have learned is that destiny is fluid, and I am absolutely elated that it has brought me once more into the lap of Mother India.

Chapter 8

Getting beyond Babel

"Get beyond Babel" is an emotional plea for the preservation of the diversity of culture and language throughout the world. The writer, Ken Wiwa, has refuted the widely accepted conclusion that we are in danger of losing cultural diversity by showing that language cannot be frozen in time; rather it is constantly evolving and assimilating into something new. The fact that approximately half of the world's 6800 languages face extinction does not imply that all of these languages will have their roots preserved in new languages. This is definitely not the case, and the author has oversimplified this point somewhat; cultural roots will be lost forever when the tree of heritage is chopped down. While language along with life is in constant flux, flux can occur in both positive and negative states.

While the author has made it clear that both language and culture are in constant flux, greater detail needs to be examined as to the reasons for the increasing loss of both cultural and linguistic diversity throughout the world. By examining his own experiences as a member of the Ogoni tribe of Southern Nigeria, he attributes socioeconomic realities as the main threat to the preservation of the

Ogoni culture and language. He argues that it is extremely difficult for a people to retain the natural ways of life their ancestors have been living for thousands of years. The irresponsible oil exploration to which the author refers has routinely damaged communities such as his own throughout the third world.

As members of wealthy nations it is our responsibility to address the plight of the defenceless. If the people of developing nations were able to grow up in their own heritage, and learn their own culture and language, then we would be more likely to see languages preserved throughout the world, while still themselves evolving of their own accord to accommodate advancements in global communications technology.

The author speaks of the young folk increasingly leaving the community to search for better opportunities in the English speaking countries of the world. By following this exposition with an explanation of the diffusion of the English language, he is providing his own justification for English becoming the new 'global' language. Through the use of tyranny and brute force on foreign soil throughout history, the English language has evolved into the global language of choice. The fact remains that the English language did evolve into its current position as the global language of choice through the use of widespread violence by standing on the shoulders of the oppressed. I believe that the author is saying that with the position that the English language is in, one would be at a serious disadvantage if they did not have the ability to communicate with the English speaking world.

It is subtle and intriguing how the author plants a seed by asking the question: is it possible for cultural and linguistic diversity to co-exist with the unification of

English as the 'global' language? The author presented his case with objective analysis, and was on the right track with his remark that language doesn't die, rather it continues to evolve in one form or another. However, the author failed to provide models for the solution to the deterioration of endangered languages. Certainly, languages cannot be frozen in time and must continue to evolve. However, by no means does this provide justification for the extinction of endangered languages in the name of cultural unity.

Wiwa, Ken. "Get Beyond Babel". In Viewpoints 12. pg 295–298. Toronto: Prentice Hall, 2002. Print.

Chapter 9

Reflections on Solitude

"We are not human beings having a spiritual experience. We are spiritual beings having a human experience." - Pierre Teilhard de Chardin

Solitude. It is the sacred elixir of the immortals; even a modicum of this precious elixir now and again can restore harmony and balance to one's life. By solitude, I refer not to that state of being where one is alone while taking recourse in the Internet, television, movies, or even books. Certainly, these all have their place and their value but that is not solitude. Solitude, as I am defining it here, refers to that act of being by oneself exactly as one is, no frills, no extras, and nothing superfluous. This type of solitude requires an unplugging from the sensory stimuli that pervade our contemporary society.

The inane distractions that our contemporary society provides with great felicity make it all too easy for the individual to become entirely disconnected from their own thoughts and emotions; a process of self-dissimulation is occurring. Countless observations of this phenomenon are available to be witnessed on a day-to-day basis. How many times do you see someone walking down the street or sitting on the bus wearing an iPod? The proliferation of televisions is another example; they are now to be found everywhere from gyms to elevators. One can't even enter a bookstore (a bookstore!) without being bombarded by the sounds of Top 40 radio. The distractions are everywhere, and this cursory approach to life has made it a rare treasure indeed to find an individual who is genuinely comfortable in their own skin.

My tone here is not meant to be sardonic, nor my aim to be accosting, nor my purpose to demonstrate the inexorable decline of the world in which we live. My intentions are simply these: to illustrate the benefits of occasionally withdrawing from society and taking refuge in solitude---one need not become a hermit or a recluse--- and to point out the benefits, nay, the necessity of embarking on a quest of self-realization. Certainly, at this juncture, the majority of readers will be quick to point out the impracticalities of such an approach due to the many duties and responsibilities of worldly life. It is, also, precisely at this juncture that those such as myself, for whom the quest of self-realization is of the utmost import, are labeled idealists, as dreamers whose footing is no longer grounded in reality.

Perhaps, I am something of a quixotic. Perhaps, it is due to a sensitive temperament, an ability that is at once a gift and a willingness to surrender to the exigencies of my soul. Yet, it is precisely this acquiescence to the callings of my inner voice that has given me dreams and longings, hopes and joys, and has continued to propel me forward. It is, also, this self-same inner voice that urges me to share these dreams and longings, hopes and joys, with others, and that has inspired me to write this panegyric in praise of those worthy and courageous individuals who fearlessly seek the depths of their being.

In our world, spirituality has become the realm of dilettantes, those in search of a quick fix without a willingness to seek the depths. This approach epitomizes the fear of introspection that plagues the common man or woman of our day. Yet, there is an inner sanctum that is available to all, and in which very few dwell. It is solitude that is the key that is capable of opening the gateway to this inner sanctum, of restoring harmony and balance, and of providing not only clarity and insight but purpose and meaning as well. It is that all too precious elixir of solitude, the holy nectar of the gods, which is capable of arousing the inner phoenix that resides latent within each and every one of us and is only waiting to rise from the ashes, to spread its wings, and to soar.

http://en.wikiquote.org/wiki/Pierre_Teilhard_de_Chardin

Chapter 10

Sonya Kovalevsky: A Biography

Sonya Kovalevsky was one of the greatest mathematicians of the 19th century, and is described as the greatest female mathematician since Hypatia of Alexandria in the 4th century. Sonya is best known for the Cauchy-Kovalevsky theorem which is integral to the field of partial differential equations. She was also a talented author and wrote the powerful novel "The Sisters Rajevski" which was based upon accounts of her own life, and is considered an accurate portrayal of the life of the Russian intelligentsia at the time.

Sonya was born on January 15th, 1850 in Moscow, Russia, and her family belonged to the privileged social elite. Her father was a military officer and landholder while her mother was an accomplished musician. However, being born in this situation limited her possibility for intellectual growth as it did for most women in the 1800s. Sonya learned science and mathematics at a very early age from her self-educated uncle; he taught her to play chess as well as techniques for squaring the circle and solving asymptotes.

When she was eleven years old, her room was temporarily decorated with some old calculus lecture notes from her father's time at university. She recognized some of the concepts from her studies with her uncle, and spent hours examining these notes, which to her were unintelligible, yet which she found extremely fascinating. By the time she was thirteen, Sonya excelled in algebra and geometry. However, her father did not feel it was correct for women to learn these subjects so he stopped her mathematical instruction. Sonya did not conform easily, however, and she borrowed an algebra book from one of her tutors, continuing to study secretly by night.

By the time Sonya was fourteen, her family's neighbour gave them a copy of an elementary physics textbook he had written, and it is while reading this that Sonya encountered trigonometry for the first time. In order to understand the trigonometric identities, Sonya substituted a chord for sine and everything worked for small angles. She had rediscovered the method for deriving the sine law. Her neighbour, the professor, was so impressed by Sonya's ability that he tried to convince her father to arrange some serious mathematical training for her. After four years, her father agreed to allow Sonya to take courses in analytical geometry and calculus in St. Petersburg. She quickly mastered the concepts in one winter; it seems that she was quite familiar with much of the material, as it adorned the walls of her childhood bedroom.

In the nineteenth century, Russian universities were closed to women, and Sonya received difficult treatment from the academic community. While Swiss and German universities admitted some women, women were not permitted to go abroad alone, and thus Sonya found herself stranded in Russia. For this reason, Sonya married Vladimir Kovalevsky, a young palaeontologist, in order that she may be free to study mathematics and science at Heidelberg, a prestigious German university. However, there she was not permitted to attend lectures, but with the help of the academicians at Heidelberg she was sent to the most renowned mathematician in Germany at the time, Karl Weierstrass at the University of Berlin.

Women were not permitted to even attend lectures at the University of Berlin, and this barred Sonya from being able to advance her studies. She was, however, determined and approached Weierstrass seeking help. Weierstrass challenged her with several problems he had prepared for his brighter students, with the expectation that Ms. Kovalevsky would not return. To the surprise of Dr. Weierstrass, she completed a set of unique solutions to all of the problems he had assigned her. Weierstrass quickly became convinced that Sonya was the most promising and the brightest of his students. He then taught her privately, and shared not only his lecture notes, but also his unpublished work.

By 1874, Sonya had provided the mathematical world with three original works of her own, each one worthy of a Ph.D thesis of itself. The first was on the shape of Saturn's rings, the second was on elliptical integrals, and the third was in the field of partial differential equations, leading to the famous Kovalevsky-Cauchy theorem. Since the University of Berlin would not issue Sonya a degree, Weierstrass presented these works to the University of Gottingen who awarded her a degree based solely on the merit of her papers, even though she had never attended the university.

Sonya was subsequently exhausted, and returned to St. Petersburg where she began writing as a theatre reviewer, and science and technology reporter for a St. Petersburg newspaper. She then began to work on her first novel. For six years, she did no mathematical work, and in its stead wrote fiction while giving birth to her first daughter. However, when bankruptcy arrived, the Kovalevsky family eventually fell apart, and after this heart-breaking loss, Vladimir committed suicide in 1883. Also in 1883, the University of Stockholm, under constant pressure from Gosta-Mittag Leffler, an ex-student of Weierstrass, offered Sonya a probationary position in the Mathematics department. She gave all of her lectures at Stockholm in Swedish, and became so popular with her students that the University offered her a five year position.

The climax of Sonya Kovalevsky's career came in 1888 when she was awarded the Prix Bordin, a prestigious award given by the French Academy of Sciences, for her work on the problem of the rotation of a solid body around a fixed point. After winning this award, she was given a lifetime chair at the University of Stockholm and became the first woman ever elected to the Russian Academy of Sciences. However, the Academy did not allow her to participate in their meetings because she was a woman.

In the years from 1888 through 1891 she worked on two novels and wrote numerous newspaper articles, demonstrating her well-rounded talents. This period, however, was difficult for Sonya as she was separated from her daughter who was left behind in Russia, her sister was dying a painful death, and a three-year romantic relationship had ended. Sonya died in 1891 from pneumonia following epidemic influenza. Sonya Kovalevsky's life was an idol for those who want to leave their records in the annals of history. She lived a full life, and her efforts were later rewarded, as she became the first woman to be commemorated on a Russian postage stamp, and she has since had a crater on the moon named after her.

"Sonya Vasilievna Kovalevskaya Biography". *BookRags*. N.p. n.d. Web. 10 May. 2011.

"Kovalevsky, Sonya (or Kovalevskaya, Sofya Vasilyevna)." *Complete Dictionary of Scientific Biography*. Encyclopedia.com 2008. Web. 10 May. 2011.

"Sonya Kovalevsky" *OP Papers*. N.p. n.d. Web. 10 May. 2011.

"Sofia Vasilyevna Kovalevskaya" *School of Mathematics and Statistics, University of St. Andrew's, Scotland*. **University of St. Andrew's 1996. Web. 10 May. 2011.**

Curnutt, Larry. "Sonya Kovalevsky" *Bellevue College*. Bellevue College, n.d. Web. 10 May. 2011.

Chapter 11

A Vipassana Experience

In July 2004, I partook in a campaign of nonviolent action that is unique in comparison to others; this campaign was a ten-day Vipassana meditation retreat. Though it was set in the beautiful Kaukapakapa Valley in the forests of northern New Zealand, a woodlands paradise, the retreat was by no means a period of relaxation. The course was rigorous and demanding. Meditation itself is not a simple task; long periods of meditation can challenge the tenacity of a person's will. To provide the reader with an idea of the discipline necessary to undertake this venture, the daily timetable for the course is as follows:

4:00 a.m. - Morning wake up bell

4:30-6:30 a.m. - Meditation in hall or own room

6:30-8:00 a.m. - Breakfast break

8:00-9:00 a.m. - Group meditation in hall

9:00-11:00 a.m. - Meditation in hall or own room

11:00-12:00 p.m. - Lunch

12:00–1:00 p.m. – Rest and interviews with the teacher, if necessary

1:00–2:30 p.m. – Meditate in hall or own room

2:30–3:30 p.m. – Group meditation in hall

3:30–5:00 p.m.– Meditation in hall or own room

5:00–6:00 p.m.– Tea break

6:00–7:00 p.m. – Group meditation in hall

7:00–8:15 p.m. – Teacher Discourse

8:15–9:00 p.m. – Group meditation

9:00–9:30 p.m. – Question period

9:30 p.m. – Retire, lights out

The word "vipassana" literally translates from Pali, the language of the Buddhist scriptures, to mean insight, or clarity. My major motivation for joining this campaign of non-violent action was, in fact, that I was seeking both insight and clarity. Before being allowed to participate in the course, all practitioners had to consent to taking five moral precepts for the duration of the course, and these are as follows:

To abstain from killing any living creature

To abstain from stealing

To abstain from sexual activity

To abstain from telling lies

To abstain from the use of intoxicants

Taking a vow of silence is a powerful form of nonviolence training. No less a champion of non-violent behaviour than Mahatma Gandhi himself advocated taking periodic vows of silence. At the retreat, all participants took a vow of noble silence for ten days. Noble silence implies silence of body, speech, and gesture. The exception was that we were allowed to speak with the meditation teacher regarding our practice, or with the manager of the centre regarding our stay.

I realized how much energy is used up in speaking, and how much idle speech is commonly used in day-to-day life, and of this idle speech, much is slanderous in nature. How many times per day does the average person back-bite another? By practicing mindful awareness, we can observe our speech in circumstances when we are upset or simply not present to the moment, and refrain from using harmful speech once we resume life in everyday society.

There were three different meditation techniques that were taught during the retreat, and these are Anapana-Sati, Vipassana, and Metta-Bhavana. Each of the three methods are directly related to non-violent behaviour; however, it is the practice of Metta which has the most obvious connection; therefore, I will describe the other two briefly and then go into further detail in describing the Metta practice.

Each of these names derives from the original Pali. "Anapana-Sati" translates to awareness of breathing, "Vipassana" means to have insight, as mentioned earlier, and "Metta" means to cultivate loving kindness. Before describing the practices, I must iterate that I am conveying my personal experience, and this does not represent the views of the host organization.

Anapana-Sati is a practice where one observes the breath as it enters and exits the nostrils when thoughts enter the mind. Practicing Anapana-Sati develops one-pointed concentration, and this is central to right action. While, in this particular technique of Vipassana, one is sweeping the body, in order to be aware of sensations arising and passing through the body.

Metta-Bhavana is a beautiful practice that is used to develop universal compassion towards all beings. In Metta practice, a person begins by visualizing him or herself in a happy state, and mindfully repeating "may I be happy" in unison with the breath. The person sends love and goodwill towards themselves. The principle of starting the practice by sending love to ourselves is foundational to Metta, for how can a person who does not love himself love anyone else?

Next, the practitioner of Metta sends goodwill towards one who is dear to him; usually a close relative or friend is the usual place for the Metta to follow. After sending positive energy to this person, the practitioner allows the Metta to flow to the next person, either another close relative or friend, or the practitioner proceeds to the next step in the process, which is to send these same loving thoughts to a person towards whom one is emotionally neutral. This could be a store clerk or librarian, or anyone else towards whom one has neither great feelings of affinity nor animosity.

After sending positive vibrations to the people towards whom one is emotionally neutral, the next step is to send these same positive vibrations to people towards whom one may feel negative emotions such as anger, fear, hatred, or jealousy. By sending the same thoughts of love and benevolence towards people with whom one has feelings of negativity, the Metta practitioner develops a deep wellspring of compassion. One may, then, finish with one's own self again, thereby, bringing the process full circle. It is this characteristic of universal compassion that is central to the non-violent reform of society as a whole.

My personal experience with Metta at this retreat was that it affirmed the compassion in my heart, and, for months to come, I was less likely to be hostile in my behaviour towards others, and also myself, in general. The effects of even a single round of Metta practice can be truly remarkable. While the meditation practices were the focus of the retreat, the evenings also consisted of a teacher discourse, where a lecture of the international teacher of the organization, S.N. Goenka, would be shown. Goenka's message to the world is one that promotes morality and non-violent conduct, and he is a noble embodiment of the bodhisattva ideal.

On the final day of the course, a documentary of the implementation of the Vipassana meditation course into the Indian prison system was shown. The uplifting film was entitled "Doing Time, Doing Vipassana". The ten-day course was first offered at Tihar jail, outside of New Delhi, one of the worst prisons in all of India. The warden at Tihar was an energetic woman named Kiran Bedi, and it was largely through her efforts that Vipassana was brought to Tihar. S.N. Goenka, himself, and many of his acolytes offered the course.

For the duration of the ten days, the teachers lived on the prison grounds with their students, demonstrating trust and humaneness towards these hardened criminals. Not all inmates were able to participate as a certain screening process took place to ascertain each prisoner's eligibility; however, the criteria of the screening process remained unknown to the viewer. The video documents the change in attitudes of the prisoners who underwent the Vipassana program by interviewing many of them afterwards, as well as the teachers who conducted the course.

The ten-day Vipassana meditation course is now offered prominently throughout North America, Asia, Australia, and Europe. The personal outcome of this campaign of non-violent action for me was that it set my sails on a new course in life. Through this experience, I was able to enter the depths of my own being and develop further levels of compassion. Attending a Vipassana retreat is a must for any person who seriously wishes to cultivate non-violent behaviour in their lives.

For information on Vipassana courses and retreats offered worldwide, visit:<u>www.dhamma.org</u>

"Vipissana Meditation as taught by S.N. Goenka" *Vipassana Meditation*. N.p. n.d. Web. 10 May. 2011

Doing Time, Doing Vipassana. Dir. Eilona Ariel & Ayelet Menahemi. Perf. Kiran Bedi. Karuna Films, 1997. DVD.

Chapter 12

The Corporate Era of Yoga

The word "yoga" broadly defines a set of ancient spiritual practices originating in India, and is derived from the Sanskrit root "yuj" meaning to join. The practice of yoga was originally seen as a method to achieve union of the Atman, the individual soul, with Brahman, the supreme soul. The popularization of yoga in modern society has commercialized this ancient spiritual practice and many corporations have tarnished its sanctity.

One major offender is Lululemon Athletica, founded in 1998 out of Vancouver, British Columbia by Chip Wilson. Lululemon aligns its product with its consumers' needs to attain inner peace, or union, and thus attributes mystical characteristics to its high-end line of yoga accessories. Yoga, with its longstanding reputation for serenity, often falls prey to this type of commodity fetishism. Any line of products associated with this ancient spiritual practice would automatically attain a degree of its mystical character.

A central slogan to the manifesto of Lululemon Athletica is that "friends are more important than money." This phrase expressly uses natural feelings such as benevolence to excuse the outrageous prices of their product line. Lululemon women's yoga pants range from $ 94 and up, while their men's yoga pants begin at $ 98. Their women's yoga tops begin at $ 48, and their men's yoga shirts begin at $ 54. These prices are far higher than those of their competitors, and it is their widespread appeal to the avid practitioners of yoga burgeoning among the affluent sectors that allows for the development of this stark contrast.

Lululemon maintains its image of authenticity by unifying its product with the convention of inner peace that yoga provides its devotees. Their stores not only distribute the yoga apparel but, also, offer yoga classes for their customers, and free yoga classes for employees. On July 27, 2007, Chip Wilson, the founder of Lululemon, rang the opening bell at the Nasdaq stock exchange while many of his associates practiced yoga outside of the building, in earnest ushering in the era of corporate yoga.

"The Paths of Yoga – Unity in Diversity" *The Big Volcano*. Big Volcano Tourism, Marketing, and Media. 1 Nov. 2010. Web. 13 May. 2011.

"Lululemon Athletica: Our Company History" *Lululemon Athletica*. N.p., 2011. Web. 13 May. 2011

Chapter 13

The Great Secret

The great secret is everywhere, and resides in everything; it can be discovered in both the minute crevices and vast expanses of the universe in which we live. A caterpillar crawls towards the unknown destiny that awaits beyond the cocoon; yet, the caterpillar is perfect in the very moment it is crawling up the tree trunk; further, it has already inherently transformed itself into the butterfly which it is to become. The present state of the caterpillar and the future reality of the butterfly exist simultaneously.

The paradise that abounds in the world around us is but a mirror image of the paradise of the soul that each one of us carries within from moment to moment. This paradise of the soul can be felt in the quiet moments when anxiety has passed, like parting clouds yielding to clear skies. In the precious spaces in between thoughts, we can experience true clarity, and therein lies the great secret, to transcend the mind, and to see all things with perfect clarity. This unerring wisdom, thus, requires the surrender of the individual self to the infinite beauty of the cosmos.

Beauty cannot be captured, but is only to be experienced by the select few, for whom such experiences are reserved, and who often make great sacrifices towards this end. How often do we aim to possess beauty, to grasp it firmly in our hands, and cling to that which is to be set free? If we view the world with a sense of equanimity, then this supreme beauty is there to be experienced constantly, it is omnipresent. To fully integrate one's existence with this beatitude, until the fundamental unity of life is ever present, this is the great secret.

Chapter 14

Grace

Tiny buds appear on the branches once more, the fresh scent of pine permeates the air and the morning dew rises from the ground, and into the mist of the sky. Another winter has been survived, and another spring arrived. One of the most distinguishable signs of early spring in these forests is that the elegant song of the Northern Cardinal can be heard; the Northern Cardinal sings only during its breeding season that stretches from the beginning of spring until the middle of summer. While the call of the male can be heard first to establish its territory, unlike most northern songbirds, the female cardinal also sings. The song of the female cardinal is one of the most beautiful chants in the entire world, and it is a song that will stir the ever fortunate hearts of its listeners.

She does not fly south during the harsh winters; rather, she endures placidly. She spends her entire lifetime within a one-mile radius of her birthplace. Perched on the branches of redwoods and pines, the mating partners have a monogamous breeding relationship, one that separates them from most other birds, and every year when spring arrives, the cardinals sing to reunite with their lovers.

Through this glorious song alone, the cardinal is able to rediscover its partner.

Dignified and serene, she sits and sings. Her song rises above those of her sisters, her mighty euphony eclipses the songs of the other songbirds, and in it can be heard the spectrum of joy and sorrow, pleasure and pain, compassion and grace that she endures. Grace continues to sing her song, she sings even though her chant has gone unanswered for several springs now. While the song of the cardinal ceases when they mate and begin nesting, the song of Grace has continued unanswered; in all its splendor and eloquence her song has continued throughout the length of the spring and of the summer this year, as it has for several summers past. Grace sings faithfully, awaiting the return of her valiant red knight with his black face and coral beak.

In her tiny beating heart, Grace knows that he will not return; she knows that she will not hear his high pitched chirp again. She knows that she will neither breed nor nest again, and yet she continues to sing, with the silent hope that her call may one day be answered, and that the triumphant joys of springtime will be hers again.

Grace also knows deep within her precious heart, that in his absence he has given her more than he could have with his presence. In his absence, he has helped her to find her own song, a melody that has eclipsed all other songs, a song so unique that it is only for her to sing. It is this song that was his gift to her, and it is this song that is her gift to the world. This song that she shares freely with the ears of the Earth is the highest of gifts that can be bestowed upon any, for it is the very song of life that passes through her.

Another summer passes, autumn arrives, and soon she will stoically endure the harsh winter once more, in the selfsame manner in which she sings. When the tiny buds and new leaves appear once more on the tree branches, the fresh scent of pine again permeates the air, and spring arrives anew, she will sing once more, with devotion and grace. When you hear the song of the female Northern Cardinal, know that she is awaiting the return of her lover, and, please, remember the story of Grace.

Chapter 15

Breaking Down the Technocracy: The Catalytic Role of Youth in Countercultural Movements

The role of youth in countercultural movements is of paramount importance; it is their role of challenging orthodoxy that gives counterculture its very meaning. The dominant culture du jour is often nothing more than an assimilation of the parental culture with those of their predecessors, and it is left to the youth to pave the way forth, with dissent often serving as their only voice. In disseminating the reality that youth play in forming countercultural movements, we will examine the articles 'The Social Logic of Subcultural Capital' by Sarah Thornton and 'Technocracy's Children' by Theodore Roszak. Through a comprehensive comparison of the theoretical approaches proposed by the aforementioned authors, we will be left with nothing but the conclusion that youth are the primary catalyst of social change.

In 'The Social Logic of Subcultural Capital', Sarah Thornton depicts club culture, a British youth culture that was burgeoning in the 1980s. She defines club cultures as "taste cultures", based largely on shared interest in music, media consumption, and an affinity for people with like interests. Club culture operates primarily on the social logic of "hipness" and, whether directly or indirectly, it is this very hipness that is the embodiment of youth counterculture. This notion of hipness coincides with an opposition towards, and rebellion against, the mainstream culture.

Youth often form together under shared ideologies, even if stemming from differing paradigms; while adults are likelier to form together under the umbrella of shared paradigms, despite differing ideologies. Subcultural ideologies are a method at the disposal of youth to differentiate themselves from the indistinguishable mass. Pierre Bourdieu defines cultural capital as "knowledge that is accumulated through upbringing and education which confers social status." Subcultural capital can then be seen as a knowledge and awareness of the latest trends and fashions prevalent among youth. Therefore, hipness is invaluable as a form of subcultural capital.

The media disseminates the values of subcultural capital. While this holds true, subcultural capital is not as class-bound as cultural capital; the idea of classlessness is a central tenet of subcultural capital, as members from varying socioeconomic backgrounds are admitted into the majority of subcultures. Age, followed by ethnicity and gender, are the most significant demographics involved in obtaining subcultural capital. Despite these inherent inequalities, youth culture is concerned primarily with egalitarianism, and often with romantic ideologies towards which any just society should strive.

In 'Technocracy's Children', Theodore Roszak effectively delineates the importance of youth's role in achieving social change. He begins with the observation that nearly everything that is innovative in various aspects of culture, from politics and education, to the arts and social relations, is largely the product either of youth that are alienated from their parental generation, or of the elder generation who are primarily focused on addressing the youth.

He proceeds to define technocracy as a "social form in which an industrial society reaches the peak of its organizational integration." Technocracy is primarily concerned with increasing efficiency, and attaining greater levels of affluence; in short, it defines the endless quest of rampant materialism. In the throes of technocracy, the entire society aims to become increasingly specialized in nature, and thus, technocracy remains the realm of the appointed experts. In relying on experts to make decisions, individuals lose the power to create their own realities. The disempowerment of the individual is crucial to the functioning of a technocratic society. This disempowerment is achieved through the ability of those who govern the society to appeal, for the purpose of justification, to technical experts, and the ability of these technical experts to then appeal, in turn, to the holy grail of scientific knowledge.

Technocracy is the politics of experts. These experts work either for the state, or for the multinational corporations running the state- there is, in fact, no real distinction between the two- and their sole purpose is simply to keep the wheels of the technocracy turning. Technocracy is free from the duality that the argument of socialism vs. capitalism presents, and it is this technocracy, a product of industrialism, through its unrestricted pursuit of perfected totalitarianism that is the real problem at hand.

It is the counterculture of youth that remains perpetually at the foreground of the battle against technocracy, due to the stark contrast between their values and those of their parental generation. It is the youth who, through their quixotic ideals and potential strength in numbers, must catalyze the repudiation of technocracy. The university is often central to countercultural movements; for it is here, that graduates and campus elders are able to identify their allegiances with, and assume the leadership of, the dissidents of a younger populace. The paradox lies here within, the universities also provide the very brains that the technocracy requires to renew itself, and the dissidents of today, sadly, often become the technocrats of the new generation.

The role of youth in promoting social and cultural change has now been elucidated. The individuals central to countercultural uprising must, however, necessarily possess a certain degree of social capital, in order to truly strive towards the manifestation of a utopia of their own making. As long as the technocracy subsists then, to a degree, the freedom associated with youth culture will be stifled. Therefore, theoretical approaches aside, the role that youth culture plays in redefining society's mores is inextricably bound with the moral hygiene of that very society, and can only take effect when the boundaries of that society have been transcended.

Thornton, Sarah. "The Social Logic of Subcultural Capital." *The Subcultures Reader*. Ed. Ken Gelder and Sarah Thornton. London: Routledge, 1997. 200-212. Print.

Roszack, Theodore. "Technocracy's Children." *Making of a Counter Culture: Reflections on the Technocratic*. California: University of California Press, 1995.

Gelder, Ken, and Thornton, Sarah. *The Subcultures Reader*. London: Routledge, 1997. Print.

Chapter 16

The Nature of Brahman as Depicted in the Upanishads

"The reading of the Upanishads has been the consolation of my life, and will, too, be the consolation of my death."- Arthur Schopenhauer

In order to properly understand the concept and nature of Brahman as depicted in the Upanishads, we must begin with a brief introduction as to the storytelling tradition of the Upanishads, and its importance in making spirituality accessible to the sages of India of that age. Once we have a background as to the storytelling tradition of the Upanishads, then we will examine two particular stories in detail, and their illustration of the concept and nature of Brahman. Through a cogent analysis of the Upanishads it can be seen that (i) Brahman is the source of all life, and the separation of matter is an illusion and (ii) the highest goal is the unification of the Atman (soul) with Brahman.

This merging of the individual self into the infinite flow of consciousness is the ultimate liberation, "Who sees all beings in his own Self, and his own Self in all beings loses all fear." The nature of self is central to the study of Brahman, for, ultimately, there is no difference. The Sanskrit word Upanishad can be translated as "a sitting, an instruction, sitting at the feet of a master" or "sitting near devotedly." This translation is in accordance with the spirit of the Upanishads, which embodies the spiritual insight transferred from guru to disciple. The interpretation of the meaning of Upanishad given by the great Indian sage and commentator Shankara (7th C.E.) is "the knowledge of Brahman, the knowledge that destroys the bonds of ignorance and leads to the supreme goal of freedom."

As commented by Shankara, Brahman is indeed the primary theme throughout the course of all of the Upanishads. The Upanishads also provide the most detailed accounts of the nature of Brahman to be found anywhere in the Hindu religion, and it is for this reason that we are using the Upanishads in order to unveil the mystery of the supreme. "The spirit of the Upanishads is the spirit of the Universe. Brahman, God himself is their underlying spirit."

It is not known for certain how many Upanishads once existed; to this day there are between 108 and 112 Upanishads in existence. Together, these Upanishads, "constitute, and will probably always constitute, the primary object of attention for all who would know the Hindu religion." These Upanishads range in length from several hundred to many thousands of words and were composed in different styles over different time periods, some of them are composed in verse, and others in prose. Some of them are conveyed as stories, others as direct discourses; even within the same Upanishad the styles can vary.

There is no certainty as to who the authors of the Upanishads were, nor any certainty as to exactly when they were written; however, the oldest Upanishads are believed to have been "composed between 800 and 400 BC" The Upanishads represent the pinnacle of wisdom of the rishis of India, whose individual lives and identities we know nothing about. Being the works of seers, the Upanishads are primarily concerned with transmitting insights which came to the authors directly through their own study and meditations. Therefore the authors of the Upanishads, "were not builders of systems but recorders of experience."

The earliest Upanishads were composed at a time of far reaching change in the religious landscape of Indian thought. At the time, the Vedas were the primary religious texts used by the Brahmin caste; these texts were only available to select Brahmin priests, and were highly ritualistic in nature. Thus the Upanishads emerged at a time when spiritual change was needed, and their yogi-authors paved the way for the tumult of new religious institutions to be nascent in India.

> "The Upanishads were composed at a time of great social, economic, and religious change; they document the transition from the archaic ritualism of the Veda into new religious ideas and institutions. It is in them that we notice for the first time the emergence of central religious concepts of both Hinduism and of the new religious movements, such as Buddhism and Jainism, that emerged not long after the composition of the early Upanishads."

The two stories will be recounted in my own best efforts of composition, after having read the three mentioned translations of the Upanishads. While there may be minor grammatical differences in the three translations, the stories and their messages are in concordance with one another, thus I have decided to recount a unique version that extracts the major strengths of all three translations.

The first story that we will discuss comes from the Kena Upanishad.

Once, through the grace of Brahman, the gods attained a victory over the forces of evil, but in their vanity and pride the gods thought to themselves, "we are great, it is we alone who have attained victory. Glory be unto us!"

Brahman, the spirit supreme, saw the vanity of the gods, and appeared before them, but they recognized him not. The gods then spoke to Agni, the god of fire, and told him, "Agni, go discover who this mysterious spirit is." Agni hurriedly approached Brahman, and then Brahman asked, "Who are you?"

Agni was puzzled, and replied, "I am the god of fire. I am well known in these parts, and am very powerful."

"I see then, what is this power of which you are so proud?" Brahman asked.

"I can burn all of the things of the earth," Agni replied.

"Very well then, burn this." said Brahman, and placed a straw (in one version it is a blade of grass) before Agni. Agni applied his entire might, but was unable to burn the straw. Disconcerted, Agni returned to the gods and told them, "I was unable to discern the identity of this powerful stranger." The gods then further perplexed, asked Vayu, the god of wind, "Go inquire as to the identity of this mysterious being." Vayu then approached Brahman, and Brahman asked him, "Who are you?"

Vayu replied, "I am Vayu, the god of the wind, I am very powerful, more powerful than even Agni, the god of fire."

"What is this power of which you speak?" Brahman asked.

"I can blow away anything on earth," Vayu boasted.

Then Brahman placed the straw before him, and said, "Blow this away." Vayu tried with all his might, but could not move the straw. He returned to the other gods, and reported his failure. The gods then turned to Indra, the leader of the gods himself, and asked him to inquire into the nature of this mysterious spirit. Indra approached Brahman, but Brahman had disappeared. Then nearby Indra saw Uma, the Divine Mother, and asked her "Who was that mysterious spirit, that has now vanished from whence He came?"

"That was Brahman the spirit supreme," Uma answered. "Rejoice in Him, it is through His grace that you attained victory." Thus Agni, Vayu, and Indra came to understand the nature of Brahman, and it is for this reason that they have since excelled above the other gods. It was Indra, above all others, who came nearest to the ideal of Brahman, and who understood first the truth of Brahman, therefore, it is Indra that has long since been considered the king of the gods.

There are several emergent themes, from the precedent story, that are worthy of discussion; of these, the foremost lesson is in humility. It was but through the grace of Brahman, that the gods achieved victory, and not through any merits of their own, as they themselves believed. Similarly, it is through the grace of Brahman that we, as humans, achieve our destinies; we must allow ourselves to be humble, in order to open up to truth. Pride is due to the delusion of the fleeting senses, in their vanity the gods had forgotten the grace of Brahman, and lost humility.

Another emergent theme is the unity of all existence; the individuality of the gods was an illusion. In fact, with regards to this story we can begin to see that any sense of individuality whatsoever is but the illusion of maya, and that all things are one, as the mystics say. We now begin to further develop the relationship between Atman and Brahman. In essence, the individual soul, then only exists in separation with Brahman, for existence with Brahman would negate any such consciousness of duality, only unified consciousness remains when the supreme target has been pierced by the arrow of insight.

The following legend aids in the further development of our understanding of Brahman, and it comes to us courtesy of the Taittiriya Upanishad:

Once there was a young man named Bhrigu, he approached his father Varuna and asked him, "Father, please teach me about Brahman."

His father spoke of the food of the earth, the breath of life, the one who sees, the one who hears, the one who speaks, and of the mind that knows. He then said, "Seek to know Him from whom all beings are born, from whom they live, and unto whom they return. He is Brahman."

In order to further study the nature of Brahman, Bhrigu went and practiced austerities. Afterwards, he became convinced that the food of the earth is Brahman. For, from food all things come, are preserved and sustained, and then unto the earth they return. Bhrigu then went to his father again to further inquire about the nature of Brahman. Varuna replied, "Seek to know Brahman by meditation."

Bhrigu then went and practiced meditation; he concluded that the life breath is Brahman. From the life breath, Atman is born, from breath it is sustained, and unto the life breath doth it return upon death. Bhrigu, however, was still not satisfied, he returned to his father, and once again requested, "Father, please teach me about Brahman." Varuna replied, "Seek to know Brahman by meditation. Meditation is Brahman."

Bhrigu went and practiced meditation. He then came to the realization that the intellect (perception in one text) is Brahman. From the intellect the world of fleeting senses is born, from the intellect it is sustained, and unto the intellect does the world of fleeting senses return. Yet, this insight did not satisfy Bhrigu he went once more to his father and requested, "Father, please teach me about Brahman." Varuna replied, "Seek to know Brahman by meditation. Meditation is Brahman."

Bhrigu went and practiced meditation. This time he saw that Brahman is joy. From joy all beings have been illuminated, by joy the illumination is sustained, and unto joy does illumination return.

This story reveals much about the nature of Brahman, we can note the relationship in this story between Brahman and the role of the Hindu trinity of gods, Brahma, Vishnu, and Siva. In the Hindu trinity, Brahma is the creator of life, Vishnu is the sustainer of life, and Siva is the destroyer of life; here, Brahman encompasses all three of these roles. When Varuna tells his son Bhrigu, "Seek to know Him from whom all beings are born, from whom they all live, and unto whom they all return. He is Brahman," Varuna is saying, seek to know the unification of the roles of Brahma, Vishnu, and Siva, seek to know the creator, sustainer, and destroyer, as the one supreme being.

Furthermore, we can see that each time that Bhrigu thought he knew what Brahman was, he was in fact not wrong at all, he just had yet to reach the ultimate truth. Brahman is food, life breath, mind, and intellect, yet, above and beyond all of these things, the nature of Brahman is joy. When Bhrigu saw through his meditation that Brahman was joy, he tasted supreme bliss. We can, also, see the path that Bhrigu took to reach Brahman was one of austerity, and this has long been, to Hindu sages and saints, the path to enlightenment. Through meditation, Bhrigu experienced the ultimate joy, the bliss of Brahman.

For the vast majority of spiritual entities, such an experience can only be grasped as an intellectual concept, not as direct reality; thus, grasping the authentic nature of such an experience can be a daunting task. However, to deny the experiences of those who have reached the highest bliss would be a form of ignorance due to an unwillingness to accept the unknown. What then do these sages tell us about the means for experiencing the bliss of Brahman? The key is simply to realize that there is no Atman, there is no individual soul that exists; for, as long as one conceives an individual soul that must meet Brahman, then this is still only the delusion of the ego. Only when one has realized that there is, in fact, no individual soul to begin with, can one climb the ladder of the highest experience, and reach consciousness of their own self as Brahman.

Experience of Brahman is reserved for the select, "Not through much learning is the Atman reached, not through the intellect and sacred teaching. It is reached by the chosen of him- because they choose him. To his chosen the Atman reveals his glory." The select are clearly those who are prepared for an arduous journey, those sincere seekers who embark upon the voyage towards the unknown; it is they for whom none other than Brahman can quench their thirst. These sincere seekers must subsequently walk a narrow path of self-discipline, "wise, self-controlled, and tranquil souls who are contented in spirit, and who practice austerity and meditation in solitude and silence, are freed from all impurity, and attain the path of liberation to the immortal, the truly existing, the changeless Self."

The concept of austerity as the highest path to Brahman is a theme that is repeated throughout the Upanishads, and is also illustrated by the story of the young man Bhrigu. What, then, are the means and methods prescribed to us by the yogi-authors of the Upanishads? The most recurrent theme throughout the Upanishads is that of the syllable "om" being used to approach Brahman. "Om is Brahman. Om is all. He who meditates on om attains to Brahman."

There are also more poetic references to the sacred mantra, "The bow is the sacred om, and the arrow is our own soul. Brahman is the mark of the arrow, the aim of the soul. Even as an arrow becomes one with its mark, let the watchful soul be one in him."

Thus, we are now in a position to draw several conclusions as to the nature of Brahman through our analysis of the precedent excerpts from the Upanishads. We know that the ultimate goal of Hindu asceticism, the unification of Atman with Brahman, is, in fact, a paradox, and is better understood as the dissolution of the Atman into Brahman; the moment the Atman has become nothing, the moment it ceases to exist, is the moment it never even existed in the beginning, it is the moment of clarity when one sees the supreme as limitless, unbounded, and as the source of all life. Everything, both inwardly and outwardly seen, is Brahman. It was only when the gods rid themselves of pride did they experience Brahman, similarly, it is only through the dissolution of the ego that Brahman may be attained. Therefore, the entire cycle of creation, preservation, and destruction is fully encompassed within Brahman; it is Brahman, the supreme, which is the voice of seeing.

Bassett, Peter. "Image and Idea – *Tristan* and the *Upanishads*". Peter Bassett, n.d. Web. 15 May 2011.

"Upanishad | Define Upanishad at Dictionary.com". *Dictionary.com*. N.p. n.d. Web. 15 May 2011.

"Isa Upanishad Quotes, Proverbs, Poetry, Folktales, Life Stories, and Essays". *Wisdom Commons*. Wisdom Commons, n.d. Web. 15 May 2011.

The Upanishads: Breath of the Eternal. Trans. and Ed. Swami Prabhavananda and Frederick Manchester. New York: Penguin, 2002. Print.

The Early Upanisads Annotated Text and Translation. Trans. and Ed. Patrick Olivelle. New York: Oxford Press, 1998. Print.

English Translation of Kena Upanishad. Trans. and Ed. Swami Nikhilananda. N.p. n.d. Web. 15 May 2011.

Gupta, Bina. *Ethical Questions.* Maryland: Rowman & Littlefields Publishers, 2002. Print.

Chapter 17

The Inventor of Chess

(Adapted From an Indian Legend)

Long ago, in northern India, there lived a wealthy king; however, despite his great wealth, this king was lacking in entertainment. He had asked many men and women to invent something to keep him amused. Then one day, there arrived a very intelligent inventor, with a large square board and thirty-two carved pieces, sixteen white and sixteen black. With the help of his loyal craftsmen, this man had invented the game of chess. He brought the board and the pieces to the eager king, and gave the royal court a demonstration on how to play the game. The king loved the game, and he offered the inventor enough rice to feed his family for ten years.

The inventor bowed humbly before the monarch. "Your majesty's offer is too kind," the inventor said, "I cannot accept it."

The inventor then offered an alternative proposal. "Your majesty, I am a simple man. I ask only that you compensate me for each square of chess in the following manner. I am asking for only one grain of rice for the first square of the board, then two grains for the second square, and then double that, four grains for the third square, and so doubling the amount from the previous square until the 64 squares of the board are filled, I will be a happy man.'

The King laughed at the inventor, "Is this truly your wish?"

The inventor bowed, "Yes, your majesty."

The jubilant king laughed, and then acceded to the inventor's request.

So it was, on the first day, the inventor took home a single grain of rice to feed his entire family. The inventor's wife, too, had thought her husband had gone mad for refusing the king's initial offer. So it was, on the second day, the inventor brought home two grains of rice, on the third day he brought home four grains, and on the fourth day he brought home eight grains. The inventor's wife began shouting abuses at her husband; however, the stoic inventor stuck with his plan, and he insisted they would survive on the rice received from the king.

So it was, on the fifth day the inventor brought home sixteen grains of rice, on the sixth day thirty-two grains, and on the seventh day sixty-four grains. The inventor's wife was beside herself with rage, and the children were starving. By the eighth day the inventor brought home 128 grains of rice, and he had now been recompensed for the entire first row of the chessboard.

So it was, on the ninth day the inventor brought home 256 grains, on the tenth day 512, and on the eleventh day 1,024; his family now had enough to have a small meal. That night they ate hungrily, and the tension within the family began to dissipate. On the twelfth day, the inventor brought home 2,048 grains, on the thirteenth day 4,096 grains, So it was, on the sixteenth day the inventor had now been fully compensated for the first two rows of the chessboard, and he brought home 32,768 grains of rice. The inventor's family threw a huge party and their friends from neighbouring villages came to attend the festivity.

So it was, by the time the inventor was compensated for the twenty-fourth square, he was to bring home 8,388,608 grains of rice, there were not eight million grains in the entire palace. The king and *his* family would now soon be starving. Many of the servants from the palace began to work for the inventor, and helped him carry off all the rice in the entire kingdom. The inventor, too, allowed the former king to work in exchange for food, and he, himself, assumed the throne. The compensation for the thirty-second square was over 2 billion grains of rice, more than all of the rice in the entire kingdom, and the compensation for the sixty-fourth square exceeded 10,000,000,000,000,000,000 grains of rice.

Chapter 18

The Flight of a Free Bird

Shortly after my seventy-fifth birthday, I was arrested on charges of political dissidence. Government officials had claimed that my writing, although entirely pacifist in nature, was dangerous and liable to incite revolution. I was taken to a high security penitentiary where I was kept in the company of a wide array of other misfits. I spent the next several months meditating and fasting within the confines of my prison cell. A short while later, I was deemed harmless, yet, they decided to keep me locked up nonetheless. I befriended one of the guards and asked him for a single favour.

I was given watercolours with which I was granted permission to paint the walls of my cell. Over the next few days, I painted ceaselessly and patiently. I painted a beautiful mountain, surrounded by lush forest and verdant foliage, and at the foot of the mountain stood a still lake. I painted a clear blue sky, with several white clouds meandering about, and a smiling orange sun setting upon the scene. I finished my mural by painting a splendid bird in the forefront, its wings spread majestically, ready for flight, and its beak held high, gazing upward at the heavens.

The day arrived, when several officers arrived in fine fashion to escort me to my parole hearing. I knew in advance, and could predict, what the outcome of such a hearing would be. After the six months of incarceration, they would now allow me to walk freely as long as I promised to never publish again. The guard whom I had befriended led the officers down the corridor, towards my cell, and turned the key in order to open it. I slowly rose from my cross-legged seated position, faced the mural on my wall, and gazed into the depths of the painting. I motioned the officers goodbye, leapt onto the back of the splendid bird, flew over the majestic mountain, and into the smiling sunset.

Chapter 19

Think Different: the use of Organic Intellectuals in the Marketing of Apple Products

"Stay hungry, Stay foolish" was the advice of Steve Jobs in the commencement address at Stanford University on June 14, 2005.

Intellectuals, even organic intellectuals with counter-hegemonic values, retain the ability to play a significant role in sustaining consumer culture. This is clearly illustrated through the Think Different campaign of Apple computers. This commercial uses the following countercultural icons to promote Apple products: Albert Einstein, John Lennon, Bob Dylan, Mahatma Gandhi, Dr. Martin Luther King Jr., Jim Henson, Maria Callas, Amelia Earhart, Muhammad Ali, Thomas Edison, and Pablo Picasso.

These icons revolutionized human thought, and by encouraging their consumers to "think different", Apple is implying that its products can facilitate this very process within the individual. Thus, using countercultural icons in their advertising campaigns plays perfectly into the ideologies of the company.

According to Matthew Arnold, in his essay "Sweetness and Light", "For as there is a curiosity about intellectual matters which is futile, and merely a disease, so there is a certain curiosity, - desire after the things of the mind simply for their own sake and for the pleasure of seeing them as they are, - which is, in an intelligent being, natural and laudable."

Arnold is illustrating that intellectual pursuit is worthwhile as an end unto itself, rather than as a means to an end. Arnold then further extrapolates upon this concept, and reaches the conclusion that culture itself is to be considered the study of perfection, "Culture is then properly described not as having its origin in curiosity, but as having its origin in the love of perfection; it is a study of perfection."

The subsequent conclusion then must be that the intelligentsia is the driving force of cultural revolution. A study of perfection would have to begin with individuals such as those aforementioned in Think Different, rather than simply with anyone who can afford an iPod. Through its association with these individuals, Apple is associating its products with perfection itself.

Antonio Gramsci, in his essay "Intellectuals", maintains that all people have the capacity to be intellectuals but not all are able to function as such within society. Gramsci creates a new breed of intellectuals, known as the organic intellectual, he says: "It can be observed that the organic intellectuals, which every new class creates alongside itself and elaborates in the course of its development, are for the most part 'specializations' of partial aspects of the primitive activity of the new social type which the new class has brought into prominence."

Hegemony can be defined as the methods through which dominant groups maintain power over subordinate groups by having them consent to, or internalize, certain values. The role of the organic intellectual can, then, be seen as counter-hegemonic in nature, as being in opposition to the ideologies of the dominant culture. From the revolutionary music of Lennon and Dylan to the revolutionary movements of Dr. King Jr. and Gandhi, these individuals epitomize the essence of counter-hegemony; by aligning their products with these individuals, Apple is staking claim to the revolutionary.

These intellectuals are the outlaws who oppose Gramsci's "deputies". As the opening of the Think Different slogan states, "Here's to the crazy ones, the misfits, rebels, troublemakers; the round pegs in the square holes, the ones who see things differently."

While the alignment of its products with counter-hegemonic intellectuals gives Apple the "rebel" image, the paradox lays in the pricing of Apple's high end products, certainly not in the price range of Gandhi or Dylan. The price of an Apple iPhone is $399, the new iPod Touch begins at $299, the MacBook from $1099, and the MacBook Pro from $1999. Each of these prices is considerably higher than those of its competitors. This natural paradox is an example of commodity fetishism, and by aligning their product with the intelligentsia, Apple is addressing the need of its consumers to think "differently".

Certainly, the intellectuals presented here excite admiration, and it is for this reason that Apple chose them to represent their product. However, despite the exalted qualities with which Apple is identifying its brand, it must be remembered that Apple is nonetheless a profit-driven entity, that is, a corporation. Therefore, the usage of organic intellectuals must, in fact, be taken with a grain of salt; for, despite the nobility of these figures, this nobility cannot be extended to Apple products themselves, even though the respective legacies of these individuals now play a significant role in sustaining consumer culture.

Arnold, Matthew. "Sweetness and Light". *Culture and Anarchy.* Ed. Samuel Lipman. New Haven: Yale University, 1994. 29-47. Print.

Gramsci, Antonia. *Selections from the Prison Notebooks.* Trans. and Ed. Geoffrey Smith and Quintin Hoare. New York: International Publishers, 1971. Print.

"Crazy Ones". Narr. Richard Dreyfuss. *Think Different.* Apple Computer. 1997. Television.

'You've got to find what you love,' Jobs says (2005). http://news.stanford.edu/news/2005/june15/jobs-061505.html

Chapter 20

Embodying Engaged Buddhism: Thich Nhat Hanh and the Practice of Peace

"Thich Nhat Hanh is a holy man, for he is humble and devout. He is a scholar of immense intellectual capacity. His ideas for peace, if applied, would build a monument to ecumenism, to world brotherhood, to humanity." -Dr. Martin Luther King Jr. in nominating Thich Nhat Hanh for The Nobel Peace Prize

The relationship between Thich Nhat Hanh and the practice of peace is an intricate web that is woven throughout the life practice and teachings of the gentle Buddhist monk. Hanh's ideas, if applied on a large scale, would indeed create a world where peace and harmony amongst humanity is bound to be prevalent, and likely to build a monument to ecumenism, as suggested by Dr. Martin Luther King Jr. In order to understand the manner in which this monument to ecumenism can be built, we must first understand something of the person of Thich Nhat Hanh. Who is Thich Nhat Hanh? Delving into the background and experience of this brilliant and beautiful human being will allow us to understand exactly from where his philosophy and teaching is coming. We will then be able to explore exactly what his ideas for peace are, and how their application would help to create a world of peace, harmony, and interfaith dialogue.

Who is Thich Nhat Hanh? A detailed background of the life of Thich Nhat Hanh will provide us with an idea of the type of person we are examining here in relation to the practice of peace. The aim of this section will be to demonstrate how Hanh is the noble embodiment of an Engaged Buddhist, a term that he himself coined in the 1950's. An Engaged Buddhist is someone who walks the sacred path of the Buddha, yet is also involved in creating social change; as we will see from an examination of his life there is no better example of an Engaged Buddhist than Thich Nhat Hanh.

Thich Nhat Hanh was born in Central Vietnam in 1926 and was ordained as a Buddhist monk in 1942 at the ripe age of sixteen years. In 1950, he co-founded the An Quang Buddhist Institute, which later became the foremost center of Buddhist education in South Vietnam. In 1961, he came to the United States to study and teach Comparative Religion at Columbia and Princeton Universities, only to be called back home two years later to join in the efforts to stop the Vietnam War following the collapse of the Diem regime. Upon his return he helped lead "one of the great nonviolent resistance movements of the century, based entirely on Gandhian principles."

In 1964, Hanh along with a group of university students and professors founded the 'School of Youth for Social Service' in Vietnam. This initiative included establishing schools, health clinics, and later re-building bombed villages. In that same year he was instrumental in the establishment of La Boi Press, which would become one of the most successful publishing houses in Vietnam. Through his works as a writer and editor-in-chief, he encouraged the warring nations to achieve peace and reconciliation. As a result of his initiatives for peace, his books were censored in both America and Vietnam.

In 1966, he was urged by the global Buddhist community to accept invitations from both the Fellowship of Reconciliation and Cornell University to speak in America about the plight of the Vietnamese people. It was here that he met Dr. Martin Luther King. Dr. King was so moved by Hanh's proposals for peace, and his initiatives for nonviolence, that he came out alongside Hanh at a press conference in Chicago and publicly denounced the Vietnam War. The following year Dr. King bestowed rare honour upon Thich Nhat Hanh by nominating him for the Nobel Peace Prize.

This fact certainly cannot be taken lightly as Dr. King was a great champion of non-violence and himself a previous winner, the youngest ever, of the Nobel Peace Prize. In 1969, Hanh set up the Buddhist Peace Delegation to the Paris Peace Talks. After the Peace Accords were signed in 1973, Thich Nhat Hanh was refused permission to return to Vietnam, and therefore he set up a monastic community in France, the country where he has lived ever since. There has been some recent controversy in the Sangha, or Buddhist monastic community, regarding Thich Nhat Hanh's return to Vietnam. "Thich Nhat Hanh has come under the criticism of many monks for returning to Vietnam in 2005."

The reason for this criticism is that by returning to Vietnam much of the Sangha believes that Thich Nhat Hanh is showing support for the oppressive communist government that is still in power there. As a result "these monks believe that the time is not right to return to

Vietnam." However, being a man of immense love, compassion, and wisdom it is my belief that Hanh is undertaking this journey in order to help to promote peace as he does in every journey that he undertakes. For personal reasons, he must feel that at this juncture the time is right for him to return to Vietnam and that his presence would be of greater help than his continued absence. To this very day Thich Nhat Hanh travels, teaches, and writes extensively promoting peace with every step that he takes.

What are Thich Nhat Hanh's ideas for peace? Before thoroughly examining this question we must keep firmly entrenched in our minds that, above and beyond all else, Thich Nhat Hanh is a Buddhist monk. Therefore, his principles for peace and his ideas for promoting peace are primarily rooted in the teachings of The Buddha. With this being said, when referring to the teachings of Thich Nhat Hanh we will refer to them as such even though many of them will be, in fact, teachings that can be traced back to the historical Buddha. According to Thich Nhat Hanh, the practice of peace begins with mindfulness of the present moment. Mindfulness is the practice of stopping and becoming aware of what is happening around us and of what is happening within us. "Every mindful step we make and every mindful breath we take will establish peace in the present moment and prevent war in the future."

This practice of being mindful is a central doctrine of Buddhism. When the Buddha was asked why his disciples, who lived a simple and quiet life, were so radiant he answered thus,

> "They do not repent the past, nor do they brood over the future. They live in the present. Therefore

they are radiant. By brooding over the future and repenting the past, fools dry up like green reeds cut down (in the sun)."

If we are mindful and aware of our thoughts and actions then "Peace is there for us in every moment. It is our choice." Hanh is adamant that peace goes beyond simply the passive lack of violence, and rather, peace requires active love and compassion,

"Peace is not simply the absence of violence; it is the cultivation of understanding, insight, and compassion, combined with action. Peace is the practice of mindfulness, the practice of being aware of our thoughts, our actions, and the consequences of our actions. Mindfulness is at once simple and profound. When we are mindful and cultivate compassion in our daily lives, we diminish violence each day. We have a positive effect on our family, friends, and society."

When carefully reading the preceding passage, we can begin to understand why Hanh advocates mindfulness so relentlessly. If we were aware of our actions, truly aware of our actions, then we would not intentionally hurt anybody, whether it is ourselves, our family, our friends, or even those whom we perceive to be our enemies. Most often when we do or say something that hurts someone else, we are not being aware of our speech, of our actions, or of our thoughts; by becoming aware of these things we can greatly diminish the violence in our lives both caused by us and by those around us. "The only way out of violence and conflict is for us to embrace the practice of peace, to think and act with compassion, love, and understanding."

One way that Hanh advocates for living a peaceful lifestyle is to avoid situations that generate fear, hatred, or negative emotions. He requests us to undertake this practice in the following manner, "Please put away any reading material that does not nurture love and understanding. Please avoid taking part in conversations that water negative seeds in you."

What better way is there to stop the trees of violence from growing than to stop planting the seeds of violence? If we surround ourselves with positive energy and minimize the sensory violence that we expose ourselves to, then we are in a position to become more mindful and to stop violence from entering our lives. Once we have made conscious efforts to eliminate violence from our lives then, and only then, are we in a position to truly become peaceful people and spread love and compassion to those around us. According to Hanh, "words and thoughts concerning compassionate action that are not put into practice are like beautiful flowers that are colorful but have no fragrance."

Thich Nhat Hanh encourages us to realize that the war begins and ends in our very own minds, "The war stops and starts with you and me." By cultivating thoughts of peace instead of violence we can stop the war before it begins. We must also be aware, however, that violence is never far away. This is why it is of the utmost importance to constantly be in a state of awareness and mindfulness; rather than saying that we will be mindful later, we must be mindful NOW. Once we do this, then we realize that peace is available to us right now, in this very moment.

The practice of nonviolence is to be here, to be present, and to recognize our own pain and suffering. We should be aware of our own emotions in this moment, recognize our deepest fears, and bring awareness to them. Thich Nhat Hanh provides us with very powerful exercises for doing this, "Breathing in, I am aware fear is present in me. Breathing out, I calm my feeling of fear."

Practicing in such a manner can greatly heighten our awareness and allow calm to sweep over our entire being. Hanh stresses that, when we don't acknowledge our feelings, violence accumulates within us; this can cause us to say negative or destructive things, and to be harmful to ourselves and to those around us. According to Thich Nhat Hanh, mindfulness is necessary in order for us to be joyful; and having joy within ourselves is a necessary prerequisite for us to be able to promote peace in the world.

Mindfulness is the foundation of happiness. A person who is unhappy cannot make peace. Individual happiness is the foundation for creating peace in the world. To bring about peace, our hearts must be at peace.

The greater levels of mindfulness that we can obtain, then the greater our concentration can become; the greater levels of concentration we can obtain, then the deeper we can understand the nature of suffering; and the more we can understand the nature of suffering, then the more we can become compassionate human beings. A fundamental basis for mindfulness can be cultivated through the five mindfulness trainings.

The first mindfulness training is reverence for life. This mindfulness training involves cultivating compassion for all forms of life and a strong resolution not to harm any living being, not only in action but also in thought. The second mindfulness training is generosity. This mindfulness training involves being aware of suffering and a strong determination not to add to that suffering in any way, and also to act in compassion towards those who are in real need. This mindfulness training involves refraining from coveting possessions and from stealing from others, as well as preventing others from profiting from human suffering and exploitation of the earth. The third mindfulness training is sexual responsibility. This mindfulness training involves awareness of the suffering caused by sexual misconduct and the determination not to engage in sexual relations without love and long-term commitment to the relationship. The fourth mindfulness training is deep listening and loving speech. This mindfulness training involves speaking with love and only speaking the truth, as well as speaking words that inspire hope, joy, and confidence in others. It also involves listening to others without judgment or condemnation, rather, listening mindfully and lovingly simply for the sake of listening. This mindfulness training is of the utmost importance on all levels of society, "In schools, in Congress, in city halls, in statehouses, we need people capable of practicing deep listening and loving speech." The fifth mindfulness training is mindfulness of consumption. This mindfulness training involves only eating, drinking and consuming items that preserve peace and well being within the body and mind, as well as not engaging in sensory violence through means such as certain television programs, magazines, and even conversations.

One of the most important methods Hanh advocates for increasing mindfulness and awareness is that of conscious breathing. It is widely believed that conscious breathing is the technique that was practiced by the historical Buddha in order to gain enlightenment. There are many different ways in which conscious breathing can be practiced. Thich Nhat Hanh gives us several simple yet profound methods that can be used in order to help us become more aware and mindful. One such method is to mentally repeat the following:

"Breathing in, I calm my body.
Breathing out, I smile.
Dwelling in the present moment,
I know this is a wonderful moment!"

This technique can be simplified to mentally repeating 'breathe in calm, breathe out smile' or even the word 'calm' with each in-breath and 'smile' with each out-breath. The most important thing when practicing conscious breathing is to be aware of the in-breath and the out-breath. This technique is at once simple and profound, as it allows the practitioner to slow down to the moment and to smile. The importance of smiling cannot be understated.

According to Hanh, every time we smile away our irritation and anger a victory for humanity has been achieved. Smiling benefits everyone around us not just ourselves. "The source of a true smile is an awakened mind." Thich Nhat Hanh invites us to hang a reminder in our rooms to smile when we wake up. This reminder can be a branch, a leaf, a painting, or some inspiring words. It can be anything as long as it carries the message to us to smile upon waking. We can hang this reminder in the window, above the bed, or anywhere we will notice it upon waking. Smiling to begin the day can help us to approach the day with calm, serenity, and inner joy. After we develop the practice of smiling upon waking we will no longer need a reminder; it will become a natural part of our daily lives. When we smile, we relax hundreds of muscles in our face.

According to Hanh, someone who is wearing a smile is showing a sign that they are masters of themselves. "When I see someone smile, I know immediately that he or she is dwelling in awareness." All of our daily activities, including eating and walking, can be practiced in a heightened state of mindfulness and awareness. On one occasion, Thich Nhat Hanh asked some children the following question, what is the purpose of eating breakfast? One child replied that it was to get energy for the day. Another replied that the purpose of eating breakfast is to eat breakfast. Hanh thinks the second child is more correct.

When we are eating we should be aware of eating and we should eat for no other reason than simply to eat. Eating in mindfulness is an important practice and should be done slowly while appreciating the food. Thich Nhat Hanh does not say that when eating with others we should not have conversation, rather, while eating we should refrain from talking about subjects that are detrimental to our awareness. Walking mindfully is another very important Buddhist practice. When we are walking we should be completely aware of the contact between our feet and the earth and of each movement that we are making. "Walk as if you are kissing the earth with your feet."

Thich Nhat Hanh offers a story about a peace walk that he was involved with in 1981 in New York City. The peace walk was happening on the day that the United Nations decided to pass a resolution on disarmament; half a million people joined in this peace walk. When Thich Nhat Hanh was asked to participate he agreed on the condition that he could walk in the style of walking meditation. Thich Nhat Hanh's group included about fifty other people from various spiritual traditions. They held a banner reading 'reverence for life' and walked mindfully through the streets of Manhattan.

All around them large groups of people were walking quickly and shouting slogans denouncing nuclear weapons and demanding disarmament. Hanh's group simply continued to walk slowly and mindfully in complete silence. Hanh later learned that due to the slow pace of his group approximately 300,000 people were slowed down. People walking behind this mindful procession yelled things like 'Can't you walk any faster?' at Hanh's group out of complete frustration. The group simply continued to walk mindfully, slowly, and silently. Then, as Thich Nhat Hanh recounts, a strange thing happened, as people passed his group and looked back in anger and frustration they themselves calmed down and began to walk more slowly. Thus the walk ended up being a real peace walk. "There is no walk for peace; peace must be the walk."

At this juncture we have now reached the heart of the matter. How would the application of these ideas help to create a world of peace, harmony, and interfaith dialogue? The key to what makes Thich Nhat Hanh's ideas and methods so powerful is their ability to affect change on an individual level. The moment when people can be mindful of their own thoughts and actions, then and only then, are they in a position to truly affect change on a societal and even global level. By living in mindfulness, people are able to consciously channel their energy in ways that will promote love and peace, and will minimize harm and suffering in their own lives.

Thich Nhat Hanh's teachings are unique in that they represent classical Buddhist teachings in a manner that is easily applicable to modern society. Societal change cannot occur without individual change, as a society is nothing but the product of choices made by a group of individuals.

If we transform our individual consciousness, we begin the process of changing the collective consciousness. Transforming the world's consciousness is not possible without personal change. The collective is made of the individual, and the individual is made of the collective, and each and every individual has a direct effect on the collective consciousness.

By changing ourselves we are changing the planet. By being mindful and promoting love and peace in each moment of our own lives, we are promoting love and peace on the entire planet and achieving a victory for the human race. This is the foundation of Thich Nhat Hanh's teaching and this is the reason why Martin Luther King Jr. said that Thich Nhat Hanh's 'ideas for peace, if applied, would build a monument to ecumenism, to world brotherhood, to humanity.'

King, Martin Luther, Jr. "Martin Luther King, Jr – Letter to the Nobel Institution" *The Mindfulness Bell*. United Buddhist Church, 1999. Web. May 23rd, 2011.

Hanh, Thich Nhat. *Peace Is Every Step: The Path of Mindfulness in Everyday Life.* **Ed. Arnold Kotler. New York: Bantam, 1991. Print.**

Hanh, Thich Nhat. *Creating True Peace: Ending Violence in Yourself, Your Family, Your Community, and the World.* **New York: Free Press, 2003. Print.**

Stahl, Bob, and Elisha Goldstein. *A Mindfulness-Based Stress Reduction Workbook*. **Oakland: New Harbinger Publications, 2010. Print.**

Rahula, Walpola. *What the Buddha Taught*. New York: Grove Press, 1974. Print.

Chapter 21

Carpe Diem

As a young boy, Johnny enjoyed nothing more than playing outdoors, and wandering through the wilderness. He enjoyed allowing his imagination to roam freely. The world of trees and insects, of salamanders and garter snakes, this was where his heart rest. Yet, every day after school, he was made to come straight home.

"Do your homework and study really hard Johnny," his parents used to tell him, "Then you will get good grades, enter into a really good high school, and you will soon be happy."

Johnny listened to them, and every day, straight after school, he returned home to study so that he could get good grades, go to a good high school, and then be happy.

The years passed, and Johnny entered high school. He had excelled in his earlier years of school, and was noted as a gifted child, and a top scholar. Now that he was in high school, rather than spending time with the trees, Johnny enjoyed hanging out with his friends. However, his parents and teachers used to always tell him: "Johnny focus your energy on your studies. If you get good grades, and do well in high school, then you will be able to attend your university of choice, and this will make you truly happy."

So Johnny listened to them, he spent little time with his friends, and instead he focused intensely on his studies, in order that he may achieve good grades, go to university, and then be happy.

The years passed, and Johnny had now entered university. If he thought that he had studied a lot in high school, university was another ballgame altogether. While in university, Johnny discovered the joy of painting. Painting had become his passion, and many a time he would imagine all of the great paintings that would procure from his brush in his lifetime. He had a great talent for painting and was certain that he was a long lost descendent of none other than Pablo Picasso himself.

Yet, his parents and professors continued to tell him: "Johnny, focus on your studies, work hard, get good grades, and you will be able to get a really good job, and make a handsome salary. Then you will certainly be happy."

A voice in his heart was now beginning to stir, and this voice told him that certainly his parents and his professors were wrong. This voice told him that he should enjoy living in the present moment and, in addition to his studies, he should focus on painting and doing that which he loved. This voice told him to seize the day.

While this inner voice could be quite convincing at times, ultimately it was simply irrational. Johnny knew that, certainly, his parents and professors must be right, so he continued to work hard, and he graduated from university with honours, and at the top of his class. He knew that he would get a really good job and now, certainly, he would be happy.

Upon graduation from university, Johnny received a high paying job with an insurance company. The days were long but the pay was well worth it, plus, he was young and he could afford to work the extra hours. What did he have to lose? After several years of working at the insurance company, Johnny got married. He and his wife bought a house and took out a mortgage, and soon enough children were born.

Johnny excelled in his new position, continued to work long days, and to see little of his wife and his children. Everyone around him praised Johnny, and they all had wonderful plans for his future. His partners and employers, his family and friends, they were all full of encouragement and would say: "Johnny you are doing a great job! Keep up the good work, soon you will be able to retire and then you will be happy."

The years passed, and Johnny had now retired from his job at the insurance company. His children had grown up and they were beginning to have children of their own. Gradually, a silent and almost forgotten voice within the depths of Johnny's heart began to speak to him again. Johnny recognized it as the same voice that told him to paint when he was in university. The voice was faint and difficult to understand, so Johnny once more forgot about it, and he now began attending church regularly with his wife.

· When at the service, Johnny would gaze around at the other people in the church, and he noticed that it was mostly full of the elderly, many of which were his friends. Johnny wondered why the younger generation wasn't here in attendance at church. One day, after the service was over, Johnny was talking to some of his friends. Then, one of his best friends, a retired police officer, began telling him: "Johnny, it's great that since you have retired you have begun coming to church. This way when you die, then you will go to Heaven and you will most certainly be happy!"

At those words Johnny's inner voice rose from its long, dormant coma and erupted like a latent volcano. Johnny realized that he had wasted his life; he had wasted the many, all too precious years in pursuit of a sense of happiness that was always just out of reach. He had been pursuing a fleeting sense of happiness that was always waiting around the next corner.

"Please excuse me," Johnny said to his wife and friends, "but I have to go for a walk... alone."

Johnny walked until he reached the cemetery at the edge of town, and, as if possessed by some powerful magical force, he kept walking until he reached a grave that was sheltered by a maple tree and upon which the sun was shining through the branches of the maple. Johnny looked closely at the tombstone, and utterly shocked, realized that the grave that he now stood before was his very own. Written on the tombstone was a strange inscription that consisted of two words wholly unfamiliar to him, the inscription on the grave read *Carpe Diem*.

Young Johnny woke up in a fright, he had been tossing and turning all night; however, he was glad to realize that it had all been a nightmare, but a strange dream. He was thankful that he now woke up as the same young boy that enjoyed wandering through the wilderness, and playing with salamanders and garter snakes. He had, immediately, almost entirely forgotten the dream except for one small part of it that had lingered, hovering just at the surface of his conscious mind.

The next day at school, Johnny entered the classroom and sat down at his desk. He gazed up at the chalkboard before him and written in large, bold letters were two words *Carpe Diem*. With these two words the entire dream returned to him, flooded his entire being, and served as a forewarning that he must not let his life slip away into the ocean of regret, and unfulfilled promise, he must seize the day. Johnny sighed, and then smiled. Today was the most important day of his life.

Chapter 22

Why do I Write?

I. "Brahman is all, and Atman is Brahman."-
Mandukya Upanishad

Why do I write? Well, why do I live, or do anything, for
that matter? The best explanation I can give is to allow
Brahman, the Hindu conception of the supreme, to shine
through my vessel on a momentary basis. I aim to live as
a channel of divine illumination. If I write, then, that too
must be my purpose for writing. Therefore to merge the
Atman, individual soul, with Brahman is my purpose for
both writing, and living, holistically understood.

Writing transcends time; it pierces into the mystical
moment of eternity. As a writer, time, itself, appears to me
as non-linear and non-local; I am able to access memories
from the distant past, as if they were being re-enacted
in the current moment. My writing career commenced
at an early age, my teachers considered me a gifted and
imaginative writer from the time I was about eight years
old. Writing brings me back to that time, and allows
me to feel eternal. I feel like I am still the same eight-
year-old boy, and forever will be. Writing is a form of

communication that surpasses barriers of time and space; it is a journey free of any destination.

Writing is best viewed as a form of service. I certainly enjoy the various forms of writing, but above all others, it is the writing of stories that is dearest to my heart. Stories both entertain and educate, they enlighten and elucidate; stories change lives. The stories of Hermann Hesse have changed my life profoundly, and my gratitude is immeasurable towards this kindred soul. He was a spirit who followed his path during his time, and I am a spirit who is following my path in my time; yet, through the sharing of stories, our paths have intersected.

Stories have been pivotal in my spiritual evolution. In particular, "The Celestine Prophecy" by James Redfield was the domino that catalyzed my spiritual path. My aim as a writer is to write stories that play pivotal roles in the spiritual evolution of others. For, ultimately, it is a collective spiritual evolution that is the goal of life.

II. "O Divine Master, grant that I may not so much seek
To be consoled…as to console
To be understood…as to understand
To be loved…as to love"-St. Francis of Assisi

What, then, does writing offer me? If I proffer my writing to change the lives of others, what does this noble craft offer me in return? Perhaps, it is an illusory blow against impermanence, but more than anything else writing offers me a creative voice. Writing allows me to play God, to invent worlds and characters, and to explore themes through narrative. For me, there is no greater gift than the strength of being a writer.

It is the message that I am conveying that is of the utmost importance; what then must be the message? The accomplished novelist learns about the very themes they are writing about, during the very act of writing. I write, then, to explore the mysteries of life, of impermanence, of suffering, of joy and glory, and most of all of love. I write to inspire love in the hearts of readers and to inspire love in my own heart.

The short stories of Leo Tolstoy have been a great influence on me in recent times, and his stories have certainly inspired love in my heart. They have truly inspired the way I act, and I can only imagine how much love he must have inspired in his own heart by writing those stories. Ultimately then, writing helps us both to understand and to be understood.

> III. "He experienced that ordinary, but mysterious and significant phenomenon, unnoticed by many people: of a man, supposed to be alive, becoming really alive on entering into communion with those accounted dead, and uniting and living one life with them. Julius's soul united with him who had written and inspired those thoughts and in the light of this communion he contemplated himself and his life."–Leo Tolstoy

Tolstoy likened reading a book to spiritual communication with someone who had already passed away. That is exactly what writing does. It allows the living on Earth to communicate with those who once vivified a material body. Writing to me, then, is a way for me to communicate long after I am gone. Perhaps, it is vain, but it gives me great solace to know that my creative voice will echo after the physical body is gone.

I think about the way I still communicate with beings such as Hesse and Tolstoy and the Buddha; these people are still able to have a great influence on my life, and they are helping me transform my life in ways that the living on Earth are not able to do.

Who is the "I" that feels called to write? Anything less than the highest power of the universe, would make this simply a play of the ego. Therefore, the answer to this question must be light energy, it must be the supreme Brahman of the Upanishads. In writing then I am in communion with the highest powers that be.

At times it is possible that the ego still wants to write and may twist off a short story or poem; I would be lying if I said I didn't want to be famous. Concurrently with fame, however, I want my creative voice to live on. A great many writers didn't really become famous until after they were dead, they were simply far ahead of their time; I don't mind being ahead of my time. I want generations and generations of posterity to read my books.

The Upanishads. Trans. and Ed. Juan Mascaro. London: Penguin Classics, 1965. Print.

Redfield, James. *The Celestine Prophecy*. New York: Warner Books, 1993. Print.

"Prayer of Saint Francis." *La Clochette,* 1912.

Tolstoy, Leo. *Walk In The Light And Twenty-Three Tales*. Trans. and Ed. Louise and Aylmer Maude. Maryknoll: Orbis Books, 2003. Print.

Chapter 23

Got Meditation?

There is a story of the Buddha that epitomizes what it is that can be gained through meditation practice. A student once asked the Buddha, "What do you gain from meditation?"

"I gain nothing from meditation," the Buddha replied.

"Why then do you meditate?" The student asked.

The Buddha gazed deep into the core of the student's being. "It is not what I gain from meditation that is important," the Buddha replied, "it is what I lose through the practice of meditation that is of the most importance. Through meditation, I lose fear, anger, doubt, hatred, worry, restlessness, anxiety, fear of death, and many more things. Through the practice of meditation I lose these and many more things, and it is then that I am able to experience my true nature."

There is nothing to be gained from meditation; many people pursue meditation with the hopes of attaining supernatural powers or of receiving great spiritual boons or karmic favour. Yet, when one approaches the practice and discipline of meditation from such an angle they are bound to be disappointed, because they have set an expectation for themselves. The moment that an expectation has been set, then disappointment will surely follow; one has to remain open to all possibilities in the present moment.

Rather than setting an expectation as to the benefits that may be gained from meditation, it is best to practice for the sake of sitting itself. There is no higher goal, and no other end, than to sit and practice meditation. If through our practice we are able to lose something along the way, then this is wonderful. If not, this is also wonderful, for we have sat and adhered to our practice; we have succeeded simply because we have followed through with our meditation.

From my own experience, I can honestly say that I have never had an unfruitful sitting of meditation. Every time that I have sat, it has been a fruitful experience, whether it was sitting for two hours immersed in the bliss of satori, or whether I was hunched over and falling asleep, every single sitting of my life has had its given benefit. The renowned French philosopher and mathematician Blaise Pascal said, "All men's miseries derive from not being able to sit in a quiet room alone."

Again, this returns to the allegory of the Buddha losing undesirable states through meditation. All of our discontent is a direct result of the mind's constant oscillation between the past and the future. The mind, invariably, cannot exist without a relationship to the past and to the future. Try this now, observe your mind and wait for the next thought to arise, invariably the thought will be one of either the past or the future, the mind itself does not exist in the here and now.

This brings up the legend of Hui Ko from the Zen tradition.

One day, after becoming frustrated with his restless mind, Hui Ko approached his teacher, Bodhidharma.

"Master, my mind is so agitated, I am going crazy," Hui Ko complained, "please help me to tame the mind."

"Come back here in the morning," Bodhidharma replied, "find your mind and bring it with you, I will tame it for you."

Thus, Hui Ko spent all night searching for his mind, yet, he could not find it. He searched high and low, near and far, yet he could not find his mind anywhere. The next day Hui Ko returned to his teacher and said, "I cannot find my mind anywhere. It is neither here nor there."

"You see," Bodhidharma replied, smiling, "I have already tamed your mind for you."

Once we realize that the mind is neither here nor there, we are in a position to progress in our meditation. This can deal a shocking blow to the ego. We all like to think of ourselves as someone distinct, and identification with the mind feeds our false sense of self. However, in order to realize our true nature, the Buddha-Nature inherent within us, we need to proceed beyond the levels of thoughts.

A Tibetan meditation master was once asked, "What is meditation?"

His reply was this: "When one thought has finished before the next one has arisen there is a gap, is there not? Well, expanding this gap is the essence of meditation."

To expand the gap in between the thoughts, and to dwell unerringly in the present moment, this is the essence of meditation, and the idea of extending mindfulness to all of our daily activities then follows naturally. By practicing meditation regularly, we will be in a state of mindfulness in each moment that we are living. This is the essence of meditation, and this is meditation as life.

"Is Meditation just a Waste of Time?"
BodyMindAwakenging. N.p. 2009. Web. May 23rd, 2011.

http://thinkexist.com/quotation/all_men-s_miseries_derive_
from_not_being_able_to/199766.html

Hoover, Thomas. *The Zen Experience.*
New York: Plume, 1980. Print.

Chapter 24

Love: The UnExpert Lecture Series

Part I

Much of what I say today will completely challenge the way that many of you perceive the concept of love.

I would like to begin with several quotes from some truly great masters of love - children:

> "Love is when you go out to eat and give somebody most of your French fries without making them give you any of theirs." – Chrissy, age 6

> "When you love somebody, your eyelashes go up and down and little stars come out of you." – Karen, age 7

> "Love is what makes you smile when you're tired." – Terri, age 4

> "When someone loves you, the way they say your name is different. You know that your name is safe in their mouth." – Billy, age 4

"I love you." When I say these three words, every single person has a different reaction. Each reaction is different because the connotation of this phrase is different to each and every person. In modern Western society, love is a concept that is usually reserved for use in relation to people with whom we have particular personal relationships; i.e. I love my husband or wife, father or mother, son or daughter, brother or sister, boyfriend or girlfriend. We love them because they are *our* husband or wife, mother or father, etc… We only care about them because in some way we feel that they belong to us, in some way we feel that we possess a part of them. This type of love is possessive by its very nature and, in fact, isn't really a form of love at all. What our society often perceives to be love is, in fact, attachment. We think we love someone or something but we don't love them for who they are, we love them because of what they do for us. We are, actually, simply attached to the way that they make us feel.

Often the words 'I love you' are related to a romantic type of love that implies exclusivity. When you say 'I love you' to your girlfriend or boyfriend, husband or wife, you are saying that you love them and them only. This type of love is very, very dangerous and is not love at all, it is in fact desire. The majority, if not all, of human suffering has its roots in desire, whether the desires are fulfilled or unfulfilled. The real problem with the aforementioned type of love is the exclusivity of it.

Eros was the Greek god of love, particularly that of romantic love. The English word "erotic" is derived from the Greek God Eros. Eros was said to have the power of making people so-called 'fall in love' with others. He often used this power to exact punishment or revenge. He used this power in wrathful ways and what he did was he made these people strongly desire others, thus leading them to the highest form of suffering. This type of desire is endless, it is ceaseless, it is similar to drinking salt water in that the more salt water you drink the more you want to drink until you have killed yourself by drinking too much of this salt water. Cupid is the Roman equivalent of Eros. He, too, was said to make people so-called 'fall in love' and strongly desire others in order to exact punishment, wrath or revenge. So, remember, the next time Valentine's Day comes around please pray that Cupid's arrows do not pierce you, for great suffering is sure to ensue.

Part II

What is Love? Dictionary.com defines love as: a profoundly tender, passionate affection for another person. The key here is that we love the other person. We do not love them for what they can do for us but rather, we love them for who they, themselves, are. Unconditional love then means that we love someone or something no matter what the circumstances and we love them for their true nature and nothing else. We love them and want them to be happy no matter what the circumstances. Let us imagine that your husband or wife, boyfriend or girlfriend called you later tonight and said, "I no longer want to be with you, I have found someone else who makes me happier." What would be your reaction? Most people would have a response that would be one of either great anger or sadness. This is because they did not love the other person in the relationship at all, they only loved themselves and how the other person made them feel. If you truly loved the other person, then the natural response would be one of happiness. You would say something like, "That is wonderful my dear, my heart is overflowing with joy, I am glad that you have found someone else who makes you happy." Love is free and it is without attachment.

I do not share the preceding anecdote in order to advocate adultery, infidelity, or even sexual promiscuity. Rather, I share it in order to demonstrate the state of being that is required of one who loves. What is the best way to love a bird? Is it to keep it locked in a cage or, perhaps, would it be to leave the cage door open so that the bird could leave but also could fly back in if it felt like it? Richard Bach, the author of the best seller Jonathan Livingston Seagull said that "If you love something, set it free; if it comes back it's yours, if it doesn't, it never was." Developing unconditional love is not easy, it requires a certain refuge of inner strength, and it requires a certain confidence and trust in the love that is present in one's own heart. This unconditional love is a desire that we must extend to all beings. For only when we really love all beings are we truly free and able to love any single other person. This type of love also requires great courage.

The following excerpt is from The Prophet by Khalil Gibran:

"But if in your fear you would seek only love's peace and
  love's pleasure,
Then it is better for you that you cover your nakedness
  and pass out of love's threshing-floor,
Into the seasonless world where you shall laugh, but not
  all of your laughter, and weep, but not all of your
  tears.
Love gives naught but itself and takes naught but from
  itself.
Love possesses not nor would it be possessed;
For love is sufficient unto love.
When you love you should not say, 'God is in my heart,'
  but rather, 'I am in the heart of God.'

And think not you can direct the course of love, for love,
    if it finds you worthy, directs your course.
Love has no other desire but to fulfill itself.
But if you love and must needs have desires, let these be
    your desires:
To melt and be like a running brook that sings its melody
    to the night.
To know the pain of too much tenderness.
To be wounded by your own understanding of love;
And to bleed willingly and joyfully.
To wake at dawn with a winged heart and give thanks for
    another day of loving;
To rest at the noon hour and meditate love's ecstasy;
To return home at eventide with gratitude;
And then to sleep with a prayer for the beloved in your
    heart and a song of praise upon your lips."

Part III

There is a short story by Leo Tolstoy that I like so much that
I actually wrote my own adaptation of the story a while
back. In this story the central character explains that there
are three principles by which he lives his life, (1) the most
important time is now, it is always the present moment,
(2) the most important person in his life is always the
person that he is with in the present moment, and (3) the
most important action for him to take is to love the person
or people that he is with in the present moment. When
these three principles are followed then unconditional
love follows, unconditional love follows because this great
big love has now been extended to encompass every being
that one is with in every moment.

    Before I was leaving New Zealand, after living there
for nearly a year, one of my best friends said to me,

"Sameer, I am going to miss you a lot." I looked him right in the eyes and said to him, "I will not miss you… but I love you right now with all of my heart." So often we have this misconception that we must miss people in order to love them; rather, we should focus on loving those that we are with in the present moment, and when we are alone, on loving ourselves. However, when we do think of people and remember them it is essential that we remember them well. This is the best way to love someone who is no longer with you: to remember them well.

A friend of mine sent a wonderful story in an email a little while back and I want to share it with you today:

'The Sand and the Stone'
"Two friends were walking through the desert. During some point of the journey, they had an argument; and one friend slapped the other one in the face. The one who got slapped was hurt, but without saying anything, wrote in the sand:

"Today my best friend slapped me in the face."

They kept on walking, until they found an oasis, where they decided to take a bath. The one who had been slapped got stuck in the mire and started drowning, but the friend saved him. After he recovered from the near drowning, he wrote on a stone:

"Today my best friend saved my life."

The friend who had slapped and saved his best friend asked him, "After I hurt you, you wrote in the sand and now, you write on a stone, why?"

The friend replied, "When someone hurts us we should write it down in sand, where winds of forgiveness can erase it away. But, when someone does something good for us, we must engrave it in stone where no wind can ever erase it."

Part IV

For love to be present there must be an understanding of the unity of all things. Love and unity go together like the in-breath and the out-breath. For as long as one sees the things of the world as separate from one another then one is not able to directly experience true love. As long as there is separation, then this division yields to a sense of 'mineness'. This sense of 'mineness', by its very nature requires attachment, and it requires us to only care for things in relation to ourselves. But when unity is perceived then universal love is born, when interconnectedness is seen in all things, when the sky and the sea are but one's reflection, then love is born. Love is born through the realization that if I hurt another then I am hurting myself also. This sense of unity is necessary in order for love to be present. Duality and separation cannot exist with love. For love is beyond any sense of duality or separation. There is a wonderful passage from the Tao Te Ching that expresses this well: "When Beauty is recognised in the World, Ugliness has been learned; When Good is recognised in the World Evil has been learned."

We must love people no matter what the circumstance. Jesus of Nazareth said "Love thy enemy". We must, also, be able to love and have compassion for those who hurt us or who cause us harm. This is true love, and this is universal love, to be able to extend our love and compassion to those who have caused us the greatest hurt and the greatest suffering. This is highly imperative. The Chinese persecution of Tibet has been, sadly, happening for some time now. However, the Buddhist community in Tibet understands that their greatest enemy is not the Chinese government and militia that are persecuting them. Rather, it is the anger that is generated in their hearts. It is for this reason that they regularly practice loving kindness towards the Chinese and have compassion for them. We must love even those who have harmed or hurt us the most. We must love them openly and joyfully, with a boundless heart.

I will conclude with a wonderful passage from Mother Teresa, "People are unreasonable, illogical, and self-centered. Love them anyway. If you do good, people may accuse you of selfish motives. Do good anyway. If you are successful, you may win false friends and true enemies. Succeed anyway. The good you do today may be forgotten tomorrow. Do good anyway. Honesty and transparency make you vulnerable. Be honest and transparent anyway. What you spend years building may be destroyed overnight. Build anyway. People who really want help may attack you if you help them. Help them anyway. Give the world the best you have and you may get hurt. Give the world your best anyway." – Mother Teresa

Dear friends, thank you for joining us here today and remember to walk the sacred path of love with courage, joy, and enthusiasm.

Blessings!

http://www.prayerfoundation.org/mother_teresa_do_it_anyway.htm

http://www.howardism.org/thoughts/000244.html

http://www.brainyquote.com/quotes/authors/r/richard_bach_2.html

http://leb.net/gibran/works/prophet/prophet.html

http://www.naute.com/stories/sand.phtml

This lecture has been presented on the Youtube at the following
URL: http://www.youtube.com/watch?v=_ktD7-tNNVE

Chapter 25

A Limiting Question

A limiting question is a question which is relevant to the nature of being but can not be answered by science alone even though it remains integral to the scientific community. "Limit questions are ontological questions raised by the scientific enterprise as a whole but not answered by the methods of science."[1] Although science has made tremendous advances in describing our universe, there are still certain aspects of life that escape the boundaries of science alone. Science is able to define the universe in terms of physical matter but this mechanistic approach leaves science in a position where there are many concepts escaping its realm. Such concepts include that of a soul, life after death, and the history of creation. In relation to these aforementioned and similar concepts science needs the help of religion or even more generally mystical philosophy in order to attempt to answer these limit questions. These limiting questions are extremely relevant in bridging the gap between science and religion or science and mysticism.

Many of the great scientists throughout history have had strong metaphysical or mystical beliefs. From Pythagoras, whose ideas of rebirth and karma were revolutionary in ancient Greece some 500 years before the birth of Christ, right through to Einstein and even more recently physicists such as David Bohm and Joel Pribram; the connection between science and mysticism can not be ignored. Religion, however, often throws a veil over mysticism. Man has a historical tendency to use religion to serve his own means however crooked they may be. Less than three hundred years after the Bible was written, it was modified by the court of Constantinople. It is widely believed that there were sections in the Bible including references to rebirth and karma but they were removed at this time.   Another example of this interference was the modifications made to the Bible in the 17th century under the supervision of King James. All major religions have had similar histories of man interfering due to his own interests. Due to reasons such as these it is more relevant to deal with the limiting questions which bridge science and mysticism as opposed to science and religion itself although religion and mysticism are still tightly knit brethren.

One major limiting question is that of the existence of a soul. In Christianity, the soul is referred to as the inner divinity, in Hinduism it is referred to as the Atman, in Buddhism it is known as the Buddha mind. The concept of soul is widely recognized by the major religions of the world, however, science itself has not yet found a way to prove or disprove the existence of this non-physical entity. This is not to say that the scientific community discards the view of a soul. Many of the most prominent scientists of all times have attempted to illustrate the idea of a soul and its qualities.   Cambridge physicist John Polkinghorne gives his view of soul, "My understanding of the soul is that it is the almost infinitely complex, dynamic, information-bearing pattern, carried at any instant by the matter of my inanimate body and continuously developing throughout all the constituent changes of my bodily make-up during the course of my earthly life. That psychosomatic unity is dissolved at death by the decay of my body, but I believe it is a perfectly coherent hope that the pattern that is me will be remembered by God and its instantiation will be recreated by him when he reconstitutes me in a new environment of his choosing. This will be his eschatological act of resurrection."[2] This is a very intricate description of the soul displaying the obvious interconnection between soul and reincarnation. For if there is a soul surviving the physical body this implies a rebirth of some sort for this entity.

The idea of rebirth is another limiting question accepted throughout many of the frontiers of science yet science has not yet been able to prove or disprove using its scientific method. However, science seems to be on the verge of being able to prove the idea of rebirth in a way using a combination of quantum physics and differential equations. By showing that the universe is made up of electrons and that electrons possess a wave/particle duality existence it can be shown that the entire universe possesses this property of being somewhat of a shape shifter. By using Fourier equations which are a sort of differential equations it can be shown that any image in however many dimensions can be transformed into a wave and then back to an image. These revolutionary experiments may possibly be able to fit the idea of reincarnation into the scientific method. Even if it does not quite work, the feeling is there that science is quite close. The fact that we are even close to proving this leads to the conclusion that yesterday's limiting question is not necessarily today's limiting question and today's limiting question is not necessarily tomorrow's limiting question.   This   is very intriguing because it shows that even the idea of a limiting question is in constant flux as is the entire universe. A classic example of this is the pre-Copernican view of the geocentric universe. At this time the question of the orbits of the planets and the solar system was a limiting question to science. They turned to religion, and at the time religion was dominated by the Catholic Church which stated that the Earth was the center of the universe. However, when Copernicus and later Galileo came along it was clear through scientific methods that the solar system was indeed heliocentric thereby turning yesterday's limiting question into one which *was* answered by the methods of science and therefore was no longer a limiting question to science. It is my belief that rebirth and karma, longstanding tenets of many religious and mystical schools, will soon be proved in the same way.

The idea of the creation of the universe is a longstanding one falling into the realm of limiting questions. Throughout history scientists have attempted to come up with theories to explain the origin of the universe. The theory that is currently the most widely accepted is that of the Big Bang. The Big Bang is quite convincing from a physical mechanistic point of view. The idea of a Big Bang implies at first glance that the universe had a beginning, that there was in fact a time when $t = 0$. However, this prominent idea can easily be challenged within the framework of the Big Bang itself. It is quite possible that the Big Bang represents a rebirth of sorts for the universe itself. Who is to say whether our eternally expanding universe may not in fact one day collapse upon itself thereby paving the way for a new Big Bang? And what if there were infinitely many cycles like this, infinitely many Big Bangs so to speak? Various religious traditions have different views of creation.

According to the bible, God created all things through a series of verbal commands "By the Word of the Lord the heavens were made, and all the host of them by the breath of His mouth." (Psalm 33:6). According to Hinduism, the infinite God Brahma created all things simply by opening his eyes, when he closes his eyes all things cease to exist. When Brahma opens his eyes again another cycle will ensue. This type of viewpoint explains how there could be infinitely many Big Bangs or creations of sorts as opposed to time simply being a linear quantity which starts at t = 0 and finishes when t equals some finite quantity.

By taking into account these differing religious ideas science can allow itself to obtain a broader, more objective viewpoint of the nature of existence which would then allow scientists to make more liberal minded progress in defining the nature of being. This is the very essence behind the idea of a limiting question. Remember, a limiting question is a question which is relevant to the nature of being but can not be answered by science alone even though it remains integral to the scientific community. By embracing religion, science can turn yesterday's limiting questions into today's newfound discoveries, thereby broadening the frontiers of science and our understanding of the nature of existence as a whole.

Religion and Science, Ian G. Barbour. Harper Collins 1997, p.90.

Science and Religion From Conflict to Conversation, John F. Haught. Paulist Press 1995, p.96.

Chapter 26

The Beggar Man

The midday sun scorched down on the black pavement of the busy streets below forming layers of sweltering heat. The sound of seagulls cawing blended with the screeching of tires and the blaring of car horns. Vendors hollered from the street corners as they hawked newspapers and magazines. Throngs of people, rich and poor, young and old, of all colours, shapes, and sizes, came and went, entering and exiting the busy train station situated in the center of the metropolitan business district.

The beggar man sat adjacent to the entrance of the train station. His worn red satchel lay open in front of him. The multitudes rushed this way and that, all around the beggar man, coming and going, arriving and departing. A well-dressed businessman attired in an all black suit scampered by, hurriedly tossing several coins into the beggar man's satchel. An elderly woman walking with a cane and a tired limp dropped a few coins into the open satchel as she wandered along. A young woman carrying a book bag leisurely strolled by and stopped for a moment to place several coins in the satchel of the beggar. People from all different walks of life passed the beggar man and tossed money his way. Most did so thoughtlessly. The odd person, like the young woman with the book bag, would take a few moments to stop and take a pause and a breath before giving a little bit of money to the beggar man.

The beggar man observed all people with equanimity. He preferred none to any other. He observed all of these people, the rich and the poor, the young and the old, with the same expression, with the same demeanour, and with the same countenance. He spoke not and he always had a slight smile on his face. Observed carefully enough one would realize that the beggar man bore the silent smile and the glowing eyes of a person who intimately knew the innermost secrets of the universe. One would reach the conclusion that this beggar man had learned the deepest truths of life itself.

The day passed in this manner, as had many prior days and as would many future days. Off to the west, the rays of the setting sun could be seen peeking through the gaps in between the towering buildings. Dusk was now approaching. The beggar man rose slowly. He stretched his arms reverently to the sky and then gently bent down to touch his feet before rising again. He lifted the satchel off of the ground. It was full and heavy. Slinging the satchel over his shoulder he began walking down the crowded sidewalks. The beggar man walked in a slow and carefully measured pace.

After walking down several city blocks the beggar man arrived at the park. An aura of peace and serenity filled the park. Large oaks and majestic elms formed a border along its outside edges shielding it from the frantic pace of the surrounding city. The sight of greenery and the smell of flowers never ceased to please the beggar man. Every day a magnificent feeling of lightness of being and supreme happiness overcame him as he entered this wonderful park.

On this particular evening, many people were enjoying the comfort and quiet company of the flower gardens and the cobblestone walking paths that this natural gem had to offer. Children played boisterously, lovers leisurely strolled arm-in-arm, and the elderly fed the flocks of seagulls. It was as if entering the park was a cue for people to slow down and to appreciate and enjoy the fruits of life a little bit more than they normally did.

In the center of the park stood a majestic water fountain. The fountain was made of white marble and sandstone. A beautiful carving of an angelic being with wings was perched on the summit of the fountain. Water flowed from the narrow top level to the wider lower level creating a large round pool of water. The beggar man approached the fountain thoughtfully and paused upon reaching it. He lowered the heavy satchel on to the ground before raising it again and pouring all of the coins that he had received that day into the fountain. His greatest joy was to help people. He enjoyed helping people to give, for it was in giving that they truly received. There was nothing more that the beggar man enjoyed than helping people to become as free as the birds that soared through the open blue sky.

Chapter 27

The Favourite Student

Ms. Gardner was a vibrant and highly attractive teacher. More than her looks, although she was absolutely gorgeous by any definition of the word, it was something else that attracted people to her. She possessed a special quality, an intangible halo of the spirit, a magnetic aura that drew in all those around her. Her walk was as swift and full of grace as an eagle in flight. Her smile was embedded with warmth that could melt icebergs. The diamonds in her eyes shone like stars in a perfectly clear night sky. One could not help but feel a certain love and respect for this vivacious young woman.

One day, three of Ms. Gardner's students were walking home from school together when they began to argue about who was their teacher's favourite student. Each one of them held the firm conviction that it was they who were dearest to Ms. Gardner's heart. The students contrived a plan to ask the teacher, each in their own way, whether or not they were her favourite student.

The first student, Rasheed, was a boy who often misbehaved and got in trouble in his other classes. With Ms. Gardner, however, he was calm and attentive. She, in return, treated him with respect and kindness.

After school, when all of the other students had left the classroom, Rasheed approached Ms. Gardner's desk somewhat sheepishly, "Excuse me Miss, but I wanted to ask you a question."

Ms. Gardner smiled, "Of course Rasheed, speak what is on your mind."

"I was wondering…am I your favourite student?"

Ms. Gardner gazed directly into the eyes of her student then replied, "Yes, Rasheed, you are indeed my favourite."

Rasheed was overjoyed and ecstatic as he left the classroom. He couldn't wait to tell the others.

The second student, Sara, was one of the most popular girls in the school. Sara received high marks in class and was involved in many extracurricular activities. Sara could not believe for one second what she had heard from Rasheed. She knew that *she* was Ms. Gardner's favourite student. The next day after class, Sara approached Ms. Gardner beaming of confidence and self-assurance, "Excuse me Miss, but I wanted to ask you a question."

Ms. Gardner smiled, "Of course Sara, speak what is on your mind."

"I was wondering…am I your favourite student?"

Ms. Gardner gazed directly into the eyes of her student then replied, "Yes, Sara, you are indeed my favourite."

Sara walked out of the classroom with her head held high and a sense of triumph about her. She couldn't wait to tell the others.

The third student, Bobby, was an introverted and reclusive young man. Bobby was an average student but he was talented in other respects. Bobby was surprised to hear the accounts of the other two students because he, in fact, knew that *he* was Ms. Gardner's favourite student. The next day after school, Bobby approached

Ms. Gardner timidly, "Excuse me Miss, but I wanted to ask you a question."

Ms. Gardner smiled, "Of course Bobby, speak what is on your mind."

"I was wondering…am I your favourite student?"

Ms. Gardner looked directly into the eyes of her student then replied, "Yes, Bobby, you are indeed my favourite."

Bobby walked out of her classroom quietly overjoyed. He couldn't wait to tell the others.

When the three students shared their accounts they could not make any sense of the situation. Each student had approached the teacher and asked her the same question and each one had received the same answer. Ms. Gardner had told each of the three students that they indeed were her favourite. How could this be? The students had decided that they would settle this matter once and for all.

The next day after class, the three students together approached Ms. Gardner and demanded an explanation as to why she had told each of them that they were her favourite student. In this moment the teacher began to glow and to become increasingly radiant. It was as if she was emitting a brilliant golden light as she began to speak, "I have told you all that you are my favourite student because in the very moment that you each approached me you were my favourite student."

She looked over her students and saw that they were confused and unsatisfied but eager to listen. She continued her explanation, "There are three principles by which I live my life. The first principle is that the most important time is the present moment. This never changes. My focus and awareness is on the immediate present. The second principle is that the most important person in my life is the person that I am within the present moment. This never changes. All of my focus and attention is on the person that I am with. The third principle is that the most important action for me to take is to love the person that I am with in the present moment. This never changes. All of my focus and attention is on loving the person or people that I am with in the present moment. Therefore, it follows that in every moment the student or students that I am with are my favourite students."

The three students were humbled. They now appreciated their compassionate teacher with a greater sense of reverence. Furthermore, they realized that Ms. Gardner had told the truth to each of them and they all realized that they were her favourite student in those precious moments that she was with them.

Chapter 28

This glass is already broken

A group of American tourists were traveling through the dense jungles of Thailand in search of the legendary monk, the Venerable Ajahn Chah. After some time they finally found the monastery where the Venerable was staying and they arrived to find Ajahn Chah drinking a glass of water. Ajahn Chah bade them to sit down and then said to them, "Do you see this glass from which I am drinking? To me, this glass is already broken." The tourists were puzzled by the statement as the glass from which Ajahn Chah was drinking was not broken at all, rather, it was perfectly fine and he was drinking from it! Ajahn Chah then continued, "To me, this glass is already broken, that way if my arm sweeps across the table and knocks the glass over and it breaks I will say 'of course'. Or, if the wind blows the glass over and it breaks in this manner I will say 'of course'. Or, if a cat, or some other animal, comes along and knocks the glass over, and it breaks I will say 'of course'. No matter how this glass breaks, or when it breaks, I will simply say 'of course'. The nature of this glass is that it is impermanent, that it will break, at some given time in some given manner. It is for this reason that I say that this glass is already broken."

The Venerable monk gazed at the travelers before him who were now beginning to understand the importance of his discourse. Ajahn Chah continued, "However, once I have understood that this glass is already broken, now, and only now, am I truly in a position to enjoy and appreciate this glass and the many wonderful things that it offers me. It is only when I realize fully and deeply that this glass is already broken that I can appreciate the way that the glass contains the water I am drinking. It is only when I realize within the very depths of my being that this glass is already broken that I can enjoy the patterns and reflections of light that are made when I hold the glass up to the sun. It is only when I realize that this glass is already broken that I can really and truly appreciate and enjoy this glass and everything that it has to offer me. That is why I say that this glass is already broken."

Chapter 29

Smile

Smile. The benefits of smiling are many. One benefit is that a smile can brighten up someone else's day whether it is a friend or a stranger. Smiling is a language all to itself; it is a language of love. Think about the last time a stranger smiled at you and how you felt. Chances are that you felt pretty good. In the same way with a smile we can help other people feel good too.

When we smile we not only brighten up the day of someone else but we ourselves become happier. We begin to dwell in a state of love and inner peace. Think for yourself of the happiest people that you know. Do they not smile frequently? When we smile, we radiate peace and love and people tend to become far more attracted to us than otherwise.

While we all would like to smile more, it is easy to get caught up in the routines and dilemmas of daily life and we often do not even take the time to smile. How then can we consciously develop this habit of smiling?

The renowned Buddhist monk Thich Nhat Hanh offers some profound methods that can help us to remember how to smile. One such method is conscious breathing. We can mentally repeat: "Breathing in, I am calm. Breathing out, I smile." Personally I find it easier to simplify the technique to mentally repeating the word "calm" with each in-breath and "smile" with each out-breath. Practicing in this manner for even five to ten minutes we automatically become calmer, increasingly present, and we smile naturally. Try it for yourself I guarantee that you will be surprised at how easily you smile and how amazing it feels. According to Hanh, "The source of a true smile is an awakened mind."

Another method that Thich Nhat Hanh invites us to try is to hang a reminder in our rooms to smile when we wake up. This reminder can be a branch, a leaf, a painting, or some inspiring words. It can be anything as long as it carries the message to us to smile upon waking. We can hang this reminder in the window, above the bed, or anywhere where we will notice it upon waking. Smiling to begin the day can help us to approach the day with serenity and inner joy. After we develop the practice of smiling upon waking we will no longer need a reminder; it will become a natural part of our daily lives. We will find that love and happiness have entered our lives and are there to greet us when we wake up in the morning.

There are also physiological benefits to smiling. When we smile we relax hundreds of muscles in our face. Smiling relieves stress and tension. Stress and tension tend to store themselves in our bodies and often times can result in our neck, shoulders, and our back becoming increasingly tight and stiff. By smiling we release stress and tension thereby reducing the stiffness in these areas of the body.

These are just some of the many benefits of smiling. I sincerely hope that you will try the prescribed exercises for developing your smile. Just as a good body needs to be developed at the gym and a good mind developed by studying, the same way a good smile needs to be developed through practice. According to Hanh, someone who is wearing a smile is showing a sign that they are masters of themselves. So please, become a master of yourself and smile.

Hanh, Thich Nhat. *The Miracle of Mindfulness*. Trans. and Ed. Mobi Ho. Boston: Beacon Press, 1999. Press.

Chapter 30

Cultivating Loving Kindness

Most of us wish to some extent to become more loving and compassionate people. Compassion is a virtue that is to be developed and cultivated through patient and sincere effort. It is important not just to have compassion for our family and friends but also to have compassion for those towards whom we feel negativity. Universal love is a concept that has been advocated by many spiritual teachers throughout history including Jesus Christ, The Buddha, and Lao Tzu, to name but a few. In the Metta Sutta, The Buddha's Discourse on Loving Kindness, it is said, "Just as a mother protects her child, her only child, with her very life, even so with a boundless heart of love let one cherish all living beings."

Metta-Bhavana is a beautiful meditation practice that is used to develop universal love and compassion towards all beings. Metta-Bhavana when translated from Pali literally means 'cultivating loving kindness.' To begin practicing Metta-Bhavana find a quiet place where you can sit with your eyes closed. Begin by lightly observing the breath. Observe several breaths as they enter and exit the nostrils. Now visualize yourself in a happy state and mentally repeat several times 'May I be happy'. When doing this we are sending love to and wishing goodwill upon ourselves. This principle of starting the practice by sending love and energy to one's self is foundational to Metta-Bhavana. For, how can a person who does not love himself love anyone else?

Next, send goodwill and love towards someone who is very dear to you, usually a close family member. A parent, a child, a sibling, or spouse is a usual place for the Metta practice to flow. Visualize this person in a happy state and mentally repeat several times 'May (name of the person) be happy'. After sending love and goodwill to this person for several moments allow the Metta to flow to the next person, usually again a very close family member. Send this love and goodwill to many people who are dear to you.

The next step is to send these same loving thoughts to a person towards whom you are more or less emotionally neutral. This person could be the mail carrier or the librarian or anybody towards whom you do not have either great feelings of affinity or animosity. Visualize this person in a happy state and mentally repeat several times 'May (name of the person) be happy'. Continue in this manner with several such emotionally neutral people.

After sending positive vibrations to these people towards whom you are emotionally neutral the next step is to send these same loving wishes and thoughts to people towards whom you feel negative emotions such as anger, hate, or jealousy. Visualize one such person and mentally repeat several times 'May (name of the person) be happy'. Continue with several such people. By sending the same thoughts of love and benevolence towards people for whom one feels negativity, the Metta practitioner develops a very deep well of compassion and universal love. One should then send positive energy to the meditation teacher who has given this wonderful practice of Metta-Bhavana to the practitioner and then one's own self again, bringing the process full circle. Finally you can mentally repeat several times 'May All Beings Be Happy'. Lightly observe the breath several more times to finish your round of practice.

"Discourse on Loving Kindness". *Naljor Prison Dharma Service.* N.p., n.d. Web. 26 May.2011.

Chapter 31

The Art of Breathing

A famous meditation teacher was once asked by a disciple, "What is meditation?" His answer was, "When one thought has finished before the next thought has arisen there is a gap is there not? The process of expanding that gap is meditation." In my view this answer really captures the essence of meditation. By expanding the gap in between thoughts we can silence the mind and become increasingly present.

There are many different techniques of meditation, in this article the focus will be on a practice called Anapana-Sati which roughly translates from Pali (the language of the Buddhist scriptures) to mean 'awareness of breathing'. Anapana-Sati is a practice used by Buddhist monks and lay people alike. It is this practice that many circles believe the Buddha was using when he attained enlightenment.

Anapana-Sati, as with the majority of meditation practices, is most effectively done in a sitting posture. It can be practiced equally well either sitting on the floor with legs crossed or sitting in a chair. The back should be erect but not stiff and the head in line with the spine. The neck and shoulders should be relaxed, the hands placed in the lap, right over left, with palms facing upwards. The eyes can either be closed or if this is uncomfortable they can be open and gazing at the tip of the nose. If sitting on the floor I strongly recommend the use of a firm cushion to provide support and leverage, this leverage makes it much easier for the spine to remain straight and helps prevent slumping.

To begin observe the breath as it enters and exits your nostrils. Observe the breath as you breathe in, now observe the space when the in breath has finished before the out breath has begun. Observe the breath as you breathe out, now observe the space when the out breath has finished before the next in breath has begun. In this manner observe the breath. Do not try to alter or regulate the breath in any way. Just be aware of the natural breath. With practice the texture of the breath will change of its own accord.

At first it may be difficult to maintain awareness of the breath. The mind will wander and begin to think of all sorts of things. Be aware that the mind is wandering and then gently yet firmly return your awareness to the breath. Do not identify with the mind and the various thoughts that arise, rather maintain a state of equanimity towards them and return to the breath as swiftly and diligently as possible. Become a detached observer who is always aware and alert.

In the beginning it is best to practice for ten to twenty minutes at a time, once or twice a day. Find a quiet place where you can meditate and a time that you can commit to on a regular basis. The most important thing, and I cannot emphasize this enough, is to be consistent and regular with your practice. Do not become frustrated if you experience difficulties rather continue your practice with serenity and patience. Over time you will find that your ability to meditate will gradually improve, your mind will become calmer and quieter and you will begin to experience the essence of meditation. In the words of the Buddha, "Just as a pitcher is filled with water by a steady stream of drops; likewise the wise person improves and achieves well-being a little at a time."

"Following the Path". *BuddhaLine*. Amaravati Publications, 1996. Web. 26, May. 2011.

Chapter 32

Right Now

"But it's not now." a meditation teacher used to frequently tell me this phrase when I would recount to him various thoughts and emotions that arose in my mind. At the time, I thought that he didn't care about any of the issues or problems that I was dealing with and that he was patronizing me. However, now, nearly three years since that time, I am beginning to notice the wisdom in his words.

When the Buddha was asked why his disciples who live a simple and quiet life were always so cheerful he commented, "They have no regret over the past, nor do they brood over the future. They live in the present; therefore they are radiant." To live in the present moment, to live fully in the present moment, is the only way to be truly happy and free from suffering. All suffering has its roots in various thoughts and emotions that arise in the mind. It is our attachment to these thoughts and emotions, our identification with the mind that causes suffering.

In his book The Power of Now, Eckhart Tolle states that the mind cannot exist without a relationship to time. That is to say, the mind cannot exist without the past or without the future, any and every thought that arises will invariably be either a memory of the past or a desire or aversion to the future. Try it for yourself, watch your mind and see what the next thought is that arises.

What you will ultimately discover is that the mind does not exist in this moment. What then does exist when one lives in the moment? This is a state of pure being, a state of unbounded awareness. It is a state that many mystics refer to, conveniently enough, as no-mind. In this state of awareness one is fully conscious of the action that one is performing.

All of the actions that we perform on a daily basis can be done in this state of no-mind, in this state of pure and unbounded awareness. Whether we are eating or reading, walking or talking we are simply aware of the action we are performing at any given moment. My aforementioned teacher used to always stress this point that whatever action you are doing be aware of that action and that action alone; be present. This may sound simple enough but to be present is not an easy task by any means.

The following excerpt is taken from the book <u>Zen Keys</u> written by renowned Buddhist monk Thich Nhat Hanh;

"I remember a short conversation between the Buddha and a philosopher of his time.

"I have heard that Buddhism is a doctrine of enlightenment. What is your method? What do you practice everyday?"

"We walk, we eat, we wash ourselves, we sit down."

"What is so special about that? Everyone walks, eats, washes, and sits down."

"Sir, when we walk, we are aware that we are walking; when we eat, we are aware that we are eating. When others walk, eat, wash, or sit down, they are generally not aware of what they are doing."

The question that is bound to arise now is, "how do I cultivate this state of no-mind, this state of present moment awareness?" Begin right now; be fully present in this moment, wherever you are and whatever you are doing. Right Now.

Rahula, Walpola. *What the Buddha Taught.* New York: Grove Press, 1974. Print.

Tolle, Eckhart. *The Power of Now: A Guide to Spiritual Enlightenment.* Vancouver: Namaste, 1997. Print.

Hanh, Thich Nhat. *Zen Keys: A Guide to Zen Practice.* Garden City: Anchor Press, 1974. Print.

Religion and Science, Ian G. Barbour. Harper Collins 1997, p.90.

Science and Religion From Conflict to Conversation, John F. Haught. Paulist Press 1995, p.96.

Acknowledgements

The help of Dana Q. Shen Michael D. Coughlin, and Vinita Chopra in final editing and proof reading of the manuscript is gratefully acknowledged.